Caste and Outcast

Caste and Outcast

Dhan Gopal Mukerji

MINT EDITIONS

Caste and Outcast was first published in 1923.

This edition published by Mint Editions 2021.

ISBN 9781513218595 | E-ISBN 9781513217598

Published by Mint Editions®

 MINT
EDITIONS

minteditionbooks.com

Publishing Director: Jennifer Newens
Design & Production: Rachel Lopez Metzger
Project Manager: Micaela Clark
Typesetting: Westchester Publishing Services

To My Friends

EMILY SPACKMAN
CATHARINE AND CLARENCE BISHOP SMITH
LUCY HORGAN

Contents

PART I
CASTE

I

Childhood

I am a Hindu of Brahmin parentage, and I was born and brought up in a small village near Calcutta. Though the early part of my life was much like that of other children of my caste, I find that in attempting to describe it to English readers, I am at once in a dilemma. The narrative, slight as it is, seems to require continual interruption in order to explain the real meaning of the simple incidents of my childhood and youth—simple, that is, in the Hindu's experience. But there has been so much misconception about India, especially with regard to our education and social customs, that I am tempted to let the narrative go to the wall in favor of what a western friend of mine calls "the oriental's fondness for vague philosophizing."

Indian life cannot be understood with even moderate justice, if its constant background of religious thought remain unrealised. That is the difference between the point of view of the most humble Hindu and such a brilliant painter of Indian life as Mr. Kipling. I use the word painter advisedly, for everything that the eye alone can take in, that Mr. Kipling not only sees but completely conveys. No one, however, except a Hindu, to whom the religion of his country is more real than all its material aspects put together, can understand Indian life from within. But here is the dilemma—to convey this in a manner consistent with the western idea of what a book ought to be. I fear it is impossible. However, when I came to America, I encountered, as you will hear if you will follow me so far, an object which figures much in American controversial, if not philosophic life—I mean the "soap box." And when my western auditor sees me mounting this humble platform to quote and expound, I hope for a degree of sympathy with my effort to present a more intimate impression of eastern life.

As I look into the past and try to recover my earliest impression, I remember that the most vivid experience of my childhood was the terrific power of faces. From the day consciousness dawned upon me, I saw faces, faces everywhere, and I always noticed the eyes. It was as if the whole Hindu race lived in its eyes. As I grew up, wherever I went on all my pilgrimages and travels, I continued to feel the wonder of faces, the faces of nature, the faces of animals, the faces of people. There was a vast procession of ideals and desires moving before me as I watched these faces and behind each I caught the gleam of a thought and began to form an idea of the person himself.

The jungle is the next thing that I remember. Our house was situated at the edge of the forest not far from the town. In the evenings, after the lights were out, we used to sit by the open window looking towards the forest. I remember one evening especially; though I must have been a very little child at the time. I was gazing into the darkness outside when I saw something that appeared to me like a huge jeweled hand. This hand, with rings gleaming on all its fingers, was slowly coming toward me out of the jungle. The movement of the hand in the darkness was intense and terrifying. I cried with fright, and my mother, putting her arms about me, said: "Fear not, little son. Those are only the eyes of the foxes and jackals and hundreds of other small jungle dwellers coming and going about their business." I was overawed by the fierce power of life, and I watched in silence the tremendous black masses of dark trees with the emptiness gleaming all around them, and the innumerable fireflies flitting about. My grandfather, who was fond of quoting poetry, said: "The earth is mocking the stars by throwing out her illumination," and at last, soothed and quieted, I was put to bed.

We lived in the outskirts of a town near Calcutta, my grandfather, father, mother and my brothers and sisters and I. As we were Brahmins, we had charge of the village temple which had been in the family for generations. I was the youngest, and of an enquiring turn of mind, I imagine, for my grandfather used to say I asked more questions than any other child he had ever known. Perhaps that is why I observed and remembered many things that to the average Hindu child might be so usual in daily life as to be unconsidered and forgotten.

I remember every hour of our ritual, and there is a ritual for every hour of the day in India; the ritual peculiar to Brahmin households like ours, and the ritual of the peasant and the workman. The members of my family, the townspeople, the laborers in the field, the many beggars—each followed an intricate and age-old pattern of life, from sudden sunrise, through fervid noon, to the heavy fall of night and silence. I used to hear people before dawn making ready for the sun. In the jungle the elephants had bathed and the tiger had gone, and all the small animals had come home to their lairs. Then I heard the song birds, and afterwards the darkness rose and the sun came galloping up like a horse of flame, and hundreds of people outside our temple gates and in the streets and in the fields waited to greet him. I used to watch them from our windows when I was too little to go out alone. They lifted their hands and chanted the verses that every day, for four thousand years, have greeted the rising sun in India:

> O blossom of eastern silence, wandering upon paths dustless and untainted by the feet of man, bring thou the dawnward way, and be our advocate before the speechless God!

Later in the day the schoolchildren trooped by, their hands full of flowers. They were bringing them to our temple on their way to school, and they held them carefully, never smelling their perfume, as that would be considered contaminating to a holy offering. As they went, they repeated:

> Come, gather flowers for the temple! The wind falls like audible silence! The winged and the four-footed ones dance to mark the beat of the steps of silence.

They used to enter the temple and leave their flowers with my brother, who was at that time the priest in charge, and then they would go on to school singing:

> With hands dipped in the colors of music and wisdom, bless us, O Goddess of Learning!

This is the usual custom that all Hindu children observe.

As the day wore on the beggars would come and sing, asking for food or small coin. When I grew older I took an immense interest in these people who throng the streets of Indian towns, especially near a temple. I remember how they would sing from door to door and often stop and talk with the people. One old man who came to our house and received a bowl of rice from my sister, gave me while he was eating, this definition of truth. "If you put all the good deeds of men in one scale of the balance and the search after truth in the other scale, the scale that has the search after truth will always be the heavier. Truth is that which holds the world together. Truth is that which feeds the universe on its heart as the child is fed on the mother's breast."

I must have been still a little child when I learned to watch for the lantern man, who before dusk would come through the lanes of our village blessing every house. I used to creep out and listen to him intone these words: "O Lord, may goodness wash away any malice that abides at these doorsteps!"

In our household, my mother was the first one to rise in the mornings. She got up about five and would always sit and meditate for half an hour so as not to disturb the morning silence. In India a woman is a goddess and must be ready at all times to be worshipped. When we children were up, we would go to her and bow before her and remove the dust from her feet. Every morning I would salute my mother and my father. To my mother I said, "You are my God, my way to God," and to my father, "You are the Way, and the End. O my father, teach me to find the Way!"

My mother was a very simple woman. She did not know how to read and write. This will seem strange to western readers, but it is in accordance with the traditional education of a lady in India, and my mother being of the old school, considered that anyone who could count beyond a hundred was too forward to be a lady. She used to say: "Don't you think an understanding heart knows, if not more, at least all that is in the printed page? The heart is the king who knows all things and has all things. The head is only the palace. If your prince be dead, what good is the empty palace?"

My mother was a busy woman, for in India it is the mother who takes entire charge of the children and their education until they are ten or twelve years old. There were eight of us, and a large household to run, and my mother never spent less than three hours a day in prayer and meditation. Yet her life and personality were so quiet, her duties were conducted so softly and with so much gentleness, that as I look back it seems to me as though it must have been tranquillity and not energy that was the motive power in our home. My mother could cook and did so, for cooking is a sacramental act and is part of the day's religious ritual. At midday she would meditate and no one was allowed to disturb her, but in the afternoon she would recite to us from memory parts of the epics, the old religious tales of India. She had been taught by her mother, and her mother by *her* mother, and so on back for generations. We would listen for about half an hour at a time and then repeat what we had heard. Sometimes she would have two of us chant the lines, sometimes one at a time.

I am afraid I was more intent upon the brilliant pictures evoked by stories of gods and goddesses and heroes, than by the deep religious significance of these ancient legends. As I was obliged to commit them all to memory, however, I gradually absorbed their inner meaning, and when I grew older, the memory of my mother's face as she recited, and the intent yet remote expression of her dark eyes seemed to impress upon me the sense of their spiritual import. We have few books in India, so each mother has to pass on the legends by word of mouth to her child, and he memorizes them, usually before fourteen years of age. By that time he has a thoroughly trained memory and this is the chief part of his early education.

All through my childhood and even after I had grown up and been away on a pilgrimage, my mother would come to me when I was in bed for the night and sit beside me and ask me about everything that had happened to me during the day. Then she would say, "Now it is time to go to sleep. Have you enjoyed anything especially in the day's experience, my son?" When I would answer, "Yes," she would reply, "Well, that was God's presence which you felt." With these words she would leave me for the night.

It is well for the Hindu child to have these human and tender associations with his religious teaching, for otherwise his prayers might rest too coldly upon his young heart. We were taught many and I give this one about God as an example of their quality:

In the howling wilderness of the beginning, who was it upheld the germ beginningless? Who wandered in that chaos of silence? As the waters gave birth to land, the secret of life was incarnated in that which dwells in land and water, the tortoise. Then as the earth grew firm, the tortoise gave place to the boar, and from the boar came the lion, as the next cycle of God, and from the lion came the dwarf, the animal that is animal and man, and after that came the full man. Then came the warrior, and after that the priest, and then the prince of peace, Buddha.

Once in a great while my mother would say to me when I came to her for my afternoon lesson, "Little son, I do not wish to instruct you now; I wish to sleep. Give me your hour!"

I did not like that and would say, "Why should you sleep, when I wish to hear the epics?"

She would reply, smiling gently, "O son, you must learn to take care of your mother, because when you are a man you will have others to take care of and must not be unprepared!"

In the evening when our father, her lord, came home, he would send his servant to my mother's maid; and his servant would say, "The lord of the house, now that he has bathed and is untainted by the dust of the street, wishes to see the goddess of the house, if she permits." Then the maid, after delivering the message to my mother, would return and say, "The consecrated one will receive you before the dusk hour." After my mother had seen my father, came her evening meditation, lasting about an hour.

She had a strange healing power, and when we were sick, she would put her hand on our foreheads and say gently, "It is not. It is not. It is not." And when we went to bed restless or feverish, how well I remember her coming to us and telling us to say these words to ourselves, over and over again, until, soothed and peaceful, we would fall asleep. In a day, or sometimes two, we would be well. People used to bring their children to her and she would tell them to say the words for themselves, "It is not. It is not," and ask God to cure them. This appeal to the subconscious plays a large part in the lives of Hindu children. In India a mother will say to her four-year-old child, "Say to yourself, you are brave, you are infinite. Nothing can be added to you, and nothing can be taken away from you." Those two phrases grow into the child's mind. Again, he is taught that he must control the conscious and learn the art of the unconscious; therefore he must learn to fix his consciousness on the following thought, saying to himself, "I am free. I am brave. I am perfect."

Perhaps here it would not be amiss for me to explain briefly the Hindu conception of mind, so often mysterious to the western intelligence. For the Indian splits the mind in two. The conscious mind takes coffee at eight, the train at nine and then runs through life making a terrible racket and calling it achievement. The unconscious mind is the eternal part of ourselves—the soul. The conscious is the thing that the unconscious has apparently created to do its work. Thus if the child continually says to himself, "I am infinite," his conscious mind slowly grows into a feeling of infinity, and the unconscious, which is infinite self, gradually becomes identical with the conscious and the two become one. In India all the prayers, such as, "Lead me from the unreal to the real; from death into immortality" or "It was never born; it shall never die," guide the conscious mind to a sense of immortality, which is inherent in the nature of the unconscious. Thus in the course of such meditation, the conscious and the unconscious are merged into one. This is what is called the education of the real self; and it is surprising to find how much wisdom the Hindus have mastered, whose conscious minds have been so little instructed.

Children in India are taught religion without knowing it. The purpose of religion, or rather the purpose of life, is that we should find friendship, love and spirituality in our souls. Ritual in everyday life is like drilling in military life. Soldiers are continually drilled, not because drilling in itself has any meaning, but because it keeps the soldiers trim, and when the battle comes they are prepared for it. It is the same with ritual in relation to the moral fibre of man. Our Indian religion has no dogma, but it has ritual, which serves two purposes. One is to drill the soul, the other is to induce a spiritual experience through symbolism. The whole civilization of India is organized to induce a spiritual experience for everybody. My mother used to say: "Ritual is a flower-laden way by which you teach the young to be law-abiding."

I was taught our golden rule: "Until and unless you treat man and all living creatures with the same consideration that you wish to treat yourself and be treated yourself, you have not attained religious consciousness." Buddha says the same thing: "It is not enough to take refuge in wisdom. You must take refuge in constructive brotherhood, and you will find joy in the result."

Every evening the mother talks to the child about the things that have interested him, so that she may find out what has dominated his imagination most. After she discovers it, she tells him to follow out that dominant experience and adhere to it, since that is the way to God.

Once I asked my mother during one of those quiet evenings with her, "Does every path lead to God?"

"Yes, if you follow it out logically to the end."

I asked, "Even the path of evil?"

She said, "Yes. You remember God had a servant once who transgressed His will and fell away from heaven. This servant was Ravana. He said, 'But, Lord, I want to come back to You.'

"God said, 'Then go and do penance on earth.'

"'But I want to come back to You very soon.'

"And God answered, 'Then go and be my enemy.'

"'Your enemy, my Lord?' said Ravana.

"God said, 'Yes; if you are born as my enemy and lead men astray I will come down to earth to destroy you and save mankind, and by destroying you, I will liberate you and bring you back to heaven.'"

So my mother said, "If you could do evil like that, logically following it out to the end, even then you would find God. Never stop halfway on any path. Go on like the rivers, to the end, and you will find that in the end you have reached God."

When I was about ten years old, my father sent me to a Scotch Presbyterian school. He said, "I have discovered a Christian saint in Dr. D——, the head of the school. I want you to learn Christianity. If you are convinced it is wrong, fight it; if you are convinced it is right, embrace it!"

When my training was over, I brought a picture of Christ to my mother while she was meditating and asked: "Why do you meditate in the presence of a false God? This is the real God I have found."

She said, "I have heard of Him from others. He has no quarrel with my God. He is one of my Gods. He is another name."

We pushed the image of Vishnu to one side, put the picture of Christ in the sacred niche in the wall and burned incense and meditated before Him. My mother said, "He who brings about a quarrel between God and God is a more dangerous sinner than he who causes war between man and man. God is one. We have given Him many names. Why should we quarrel about names?"

When we quarrel about names we fall away from religion and come into dogma. Religion is a spiritual experience—and in that sense the Hindus are religious, as are the Chinese, the Jews or the Mohammedans.

An ordinary Indian boy, who was not born like myself into the priest caste, would have gone to an Indian or an English government school. There are certain schools where he could learn to read and write, but not many. There are old Indian schools where he would have studied the Scriptures. I attended school about ten years altogether, as I remember, but in order to be a good Brahmin your studies never stop. You learn even from the Christian saints.

While I was at school, I still continued to hear my mother's stories. Once I said to her, "Why do we have waves in the Ganges?"

She replied, "Don't you see? In the beginning the mountains had wings and used to fly and cast their shadows. And the stars and sun and moon grew jealous, so they declared war against the mountains and clipped their wings with a thunder bolt. Some of the mountains took shelter under the water where the thunder could not reach them. And now they sometimes fly in the water and you see their wings showing above, and thus we have waves."

I used to spend hours watching the Ganges and not a fraction of a wing could I see sticking out of the water. And other such tales she used to tell me many times.

"Why is there poetry?" I once asked her.

And she told me this story:

"There was a man avid for riches. The only way he could obtain wealth was to kill people and take their goods. His name was Ratnakar. Once he attacked a saint, and said to him, 'Your wealth or your life!'

"'I have only my life,' the saint replied. 'I am a man who believes in holiness, and I spend my life in wandering and prayer. But tell me why you try to take other people's possessions?'

"'Because I want imperishable riches,' said Ratnakar.

"The saint replied, 'All riches are perishable. Why don't you write a life of God? That will give you imperishable wealth.'

"'But I am no poet,' said Ratnakar.

"'Then you are the very man,' replied the saint. 'Go and meditate until the thing becomes clear to you.'

"So Ratnakar meditated for so long a time that the ant-hills grew over him and he was called 'the ant-hill covered man,' which in Sanskrit reads 'Valmiki.'

"One day he saw the epic poem about God clear in his mind and the song in his heart. He rose from his meditation, broke through the ant-hills and took a bath in the Ganges. Then he filled his pitcher with holy water. As he was going onwards, he saw two herons loving each other on a tree, and as he was enjoying this spectacle, a fowler shot an arrow which pierced one of the herons. The wounded bird fell to the ground shrieking, and the fowler hastened to take his prey in his hand. Valmiki, who had been a thief, but whose heart had been purified by meditation until he had become a poet, cried,

"'Oh thou low born! Thou wilt never attain ascendency in this world, for thou hast killed a love-intoxicated one! But I will give life to the bird by the miracle of holy water.'

"He poured holy water upon it and the bird flew up to its mate.

"Thus," my mother concluded, "poetry was born. The sorrow of lovers is the song of poets."

My mother told me the following fable to show that he who *is,* is greater than he who *does:*

"Once the mother of the universe was sitting on the golden throne of eternity. She had two children, the god of wisdom and the god of war. They wanted to get on her lap, but she said: 'I cannot take both of you; who will be the first? Run a race around the universe, and he who wins, I'll take on my lap.' The god of war went off on his peacock steed. The god of wisdom had an elephant's head but he had no way of carrying it and nothing to ride. He could hear his brother going at full speed. Then the god of wisdom went to his mother and sat on her lap. When the war god came back, he was, of course, very much put out and cried, 'Why do I see him on your lap? *He* didn't run a race!' She answered, 'He didn't run, but it isn't going around the outside of the universe, it is going around the centre of the universe that counts.'"

Beside the fairy tales, our mother, like all Indian mothers, talked to us about various philosophical and religious problems. We would ask her, for instance, "Why do the sacred books conflict?"

My mother answered, "Truth is one, but sacred books have tried to give it many names. Why quarrel about names?" That is the sort of thing she would say. The sum and substance of my mother's teaching was this: "All religions are one. There have been prophets before, there will be prophets again, and prophets are here. You are your own prophet." She said, "Religion ought to be like a great banyan tree, continually growing and branching out, and, like the banyan tree, throwing down new roots, so that all the homing birds of life may have their nests in it. Keep this tree growing, and within its branches and its shade all the other religions will grow their roots and branches too, and all human souls, like homing birds, will find their nests there."

My grandfather taught me poetry. His memory was going when I was nine or ten, and in order to exercise it, he taught poetry to me. Now, in the Scotch school, they gave me a book to study, called geography, and there was no end of talk about places. One day I was reading about Calcutta. I showed my geography to my grandfather and said to him, "We are reading about our own city," and then I gave him a list of our export and import trade.

"But that is not geography," said the old man. "I have it in an ancient book and I will show you." So he went and got Kalidassa's *Cloud Messenger.* He read and translated to me the following tale from the Sanskrit:

"A Titan was employed in the Himalayas by God to look after the treasury, but he defaulted and was exiled a whole year at the southern point of India. Being homesick, he wanted to send a message to his wife, but had no messenger. Suddenly he saw the July cloud rising from the Indian ocean. 'I'll send a message through this cloud.'

"So he said:

"'In the first flush of July the clouds rise; as the elephant charges the mountains with its tusks, so the cloud charges the sky with its tusks of lightning. O you born of the sun of the gods! O sun of the wandering heavens, take this message to my wife, and as you go, I will tell you how to reach my home!'

"Then he gave his directions:

"'When you come to the blue mountains, you feel the breeze becoming different. The wind caresses you. The white cranes make eye-pleasing circles before you. Peacocks stand on branches of the trees, their fans outspread, dancing to the drumming of thunder. At last you reach the Himalayas. And you will see where the rainbow bends its glory to make an entrance for the gods. You will find a woman there whose bracelets are too big for her wrists, because she has grown thin, longing for me. She is my wife.'

"That," said my grandfather, "is geography, not exports and imports."

I have spoken of my father. He had read a great deal, and used to tell us many strange tales. I remember one in particular that delighted and mystified me, about two curious people named Don Quixote and Sancho Panza. He used also to sing to us and he talked with us at all times, yet we never seemed to lose our awe of him, and in spite of our intimate family life, he always remained to us a kind of god. I remember him as an Olympian who was lost in this world, and I think he must have been dejected about it, for there is a distinct impression of melancholy in my mind associated with his tall, thin figure and delicate, aquiline features. Perhaps this was due to his ill health, however, for when I was a child he had hardly recovered from a severe illness that seriously interrupted the course of his life. Although a Brahmin he never became a priest. He was a lawyer by profession, and after his illness he gave up his practice and studied music for many years with a very old Mohammedan musician, named Moradali.

This most remarkable man would sometimes come to stay with us, and in this case we would break the laws of our caste, and my mother would cook meat for him. He had become my father's spiritual adviser, and therefore whatever he ate was spiritual. As we were Hindu children, he taught us Vishnu hymns. He was a very old man and was always telling his beads and I am afraid we used to make fun of him, but he never minded it. He had a terrific way of opening his mouth when he sang, and we used to tell him that he almost swallowed the universe. He taught my father music for twelve years. A certain rich man, a friend of my father, used often to share his lessons. One day Moradali said to this rich man, "I cannot give you any more instruction."

"Why not?" he said. "You are teaching Mukerji so much."

"You see," replied Moradali, "Mukerji is a poor man. I have given you the training of a critic, so that when good musicians come you will know enough to support them and they will be able to remain good musicians; but Mukerji will have to make his living by music, while you criticize it."

Moradali told us about the six great Indian melodies, sung at three, six and nine in the morning, and then at noon, six and twelve at night. There are also many other melodies, variations and combinations of these. He told us that the people are continually making wild melodies which violate all these fixed rules and which are called "jungli."

Moradali had a curious history. He had suffered a terrible grief in his youth from which he never recovered. He was the court musician of the Emperor of Delhi at the time of the mutiny in 1857. He was eighteen when this occurred; the Emperor's son was shot in his presence after being captured by Nicholson's men. Then the Emperor was taken prisoner, and Moradali escaped from the town where the Emperor was held a captive, a musician dispossessed of his dignity. Soon after, the Emperor lay dying and he cried, "Where is Moradali to sing to me now? I have paid him all his life." But the Emperor died before the news of his last desire could reach the musician. Moradali was in despair. He said, "I have eaten my master's salt all my life, but at the end I could not serve him!" He then composed a song which is known as the "Remorse Song."

O my king, for your sake I go as a mendicant of song from door to door, but desolation greets me as a great shadow on either hand! The glories are gone and wild animals prowl through the palaces. But the wild animals that prowl through my heart, who can take *them* away?

You can hear this song now in India. It is a terrible cry of anguish. All India knows the six o'clock melody; the world rises to it, and all the morning music that is made is based upon it. It cannot be altered. The evening melody is called the "Tiger Beauty." I have heard Moradali sing it. He would stretch his lips, narrowing them in the corners, so that they took the sinister form of a tiger's mouth giving the hunger cry. At ten o'clock in the evening he would sing his Remorse Song, always, when he was with us. And though we children used to make fun of him sometimes, we all worshipped this man.

Once I said to Moradali, "Grandfather, tell me; why music?"

He replied: "When the Lord made the universe He made men righteous, but they did not remain so. He gave them sculpture to reclaim them. They played with it for only a few hours. Then He said: 'I will give them the power of melody; through it they will come back to Me.' So He sang out the sun, and rolled out the thunder melody. (But this tune has been lost for two thousand years.) Thus music was created to bring man back to God."

I said, "Did you go back to God in this way?"

He shook his head and would say no more.

I asked my father once, "Why music?"

He answered, "I don't know, but I think this. Once on a time there were nine stars and one of them was attracted by the life of the world and fell away to come to earth. No one knows what happened, but it lost itself in everything that lives. From time to time it cries out to the other eight stars; that is music."

As my father's health became better, he renewed his practice of law for nine months in the year, but during the vacations we used to go in a cart drawn by bullocks from the court of one rajah to another, where he sang. And now that he was well and again practicing law, he had the idea that he should never take money for his playing.

While we travelled in the bullock carts, my father was always talking. He would tell us about his begging time and the Sepoy rebellion of 1857. We passed through places where he had seen massacres. One night we had an adventure with a tiger. As long as a cart moves, a tiger will never attack the oxen because the motion of the wheels frightens him. If the animals stop, however, he will fall upon them. We were all fast asleep. The bullocks stopped. We woke, missing the motion. The driver was asleep on the prow of the cart. We raised our heads and saw two very beautiful green eyes in the distance. The bullocks were shivering and you could smell fear. The driver woke up and said, "O my father, it is a tiger!"

"Shut up, fool, let us see him!" my father rejoined.

The driver stopped shouting, we looked at the tiger and as we looked, the green eyes grew larger and larger. Saying, "He is going to leap!" my father tore open the straw mattress upon which we were lying, lit a match and the straw went up in a flame. "Grrrrrr!" With this growl we heard a swift movement in the air, followed by the crashing of a branch, then a thud in the jungle. The bullocks began to move again, but for an hour we kept burning the straw until the tiger was completely frightened away.

There are 30,000 people killed every year by the tigers, but you have to be a very important man and take out a license from the Government before you are allowed to carry a gun in India.

My father, when it was possible, would travel by boat upon the rivers which ran through the jungle. Once when we were sitting on the boat we saw a boy on the river bank playing a flute and we noticed that a crocodile was creeping up.

My father shouted, "O thou great fool and the grandchild of an arch fool, a mighty crocodile is upon thee!"

The boy replied, "Oh, hold thy tongue, there is no crocodile in the river!"

My father answered, "Thou shalt see, but it will be too late!"

The crocodile came up and struck at the boy and he fell backwards. When we came up, we found he had fainted from terror. We revived him and my father reprimanded him.

He said, "I beg your pardon. I did not know you were a Brahmin. Brahmins are sometimes wise."

My father used to anchor his boat in the middle of the river at night. Sometimes we saw the tall grasses on the banks go like waves in the moonlight. My father would say, "Watch! It waves like silken stripes."

"What is it?"

"It is the tiger."

Suddenly we would see the fierce eyes of the monster on the bank. But being uncertain of the distance between himself and us, he dared not attack us. If he sprang and fell short, the crocodiles would seize him.

Once in these travels, at the court of a certain rajah, I saw what impressed me as being very royal manners. We were received at the palace and were sitting around the rajah. I was behind my father. In India they give you tobacco braziers with charcoal burning in them, and one of the braziers did not fit the rajah's hookah, and the burning charcoal fell on a beautiful old rug. The court flatterers cried, "Call the servants!" But the rajah picked up the coals one by one with his own fingers and put them back again in the brazier. When the servants appeared in consternation, the rajah merely remarked, "Strange things are happening these days"—then the music began and everything went on as before.

II

My Little Sister

My sister, nearest of an age to me, was constantly with me sharing the attention of our mother and playing with me in and about the enclosure of the temple. I remember vividly one occasion when she and I had been sent with offerings for the shrine. We were passing through the courtyard of the temple, when a monkey jumped down in tawny grandeur from the yellow sandstone roof, like a piece of the stone itself suddenly dislodged. He stood before us and grinned so menacingly that we dropped our offering to the ground in terror, whereupon he sat himself down on his haunches and began to devour our carefully selected bananas and sweetmeats. At this my sister (she was about eight years old at the time) lost her temper completely and kicked the monkey in the face. He, poor beast, screamed wildly and ran for his life. Then my sister burst into angry and remorseful tears. She stood amid the scattered fruit and sobbed. "Vulgar and indecent monkey, to make me behave in such an unladylike fashion! Oh, the shame of having kicked anyone in public!" I can see her now, a slender little figure painted on the gold background of yellow sandstone; the sharp contrast of her very long black hair; the big, black, tearful eyes and straight little nose in a round and serious face.

This sister was the youngest of our large family, an amiable child on the whole, and not given to quarreling. My mother had a good influence over us all in this respect and used her increasing deafness to much effect when any differences arose between us. When she was appealed to, to settle disputes, she used to say, "I didn't hear a thing—you must have been quarreling on my deaf side." So when my little sister, at the age of seven, invented wonderful stories about herself, and informed us that she had had a monkey for a nurse who used to give her rides in the sky every day, and affirmed loudly, "It is true, it is true; ask mother," my mother's deafness was very noticeable.

The child was a quaint mixture of impulse and reflection. She had a strong religious instinct which was, of course, fostered by her training. Her favorite occupation was making grotesque symbols of divinity out of mud. She had a small wooden stool where she enshrined the mud gods and burnt incense before them, morning, noon and night. No one god lasted very long. After a week the symbol would bore her and she would throw it away, saying to my mother, "I must make a new worship, the old one was not good and I threw it into the river."

"Yes," said my mother. "Worship, if it is not ever fresh, palls both on gods and men."

Little sister would sit on the red-tiled cemented floor in a gorgeous yellow robe, and chant hymns by the hour. I used to say, in superior, elder-brother fashion, "Why do you sit on the floor; why don't you kneel?"

"The floor is hard, it hurts my knees. I don't think the Lord likes us to endure pain." She never could bear to suffer, poor little sister, which perhaps may have been for her an incentive to philosophy.

I remember that she was very fond of ornaments and was wrapped in gloom for a week after the loss of one of her trinkets. At last one day she suddenly became cheerful again, and announced without preface, "Every woman must have lost a ring when she was a little girl."

When she was old enough to go to school, she was sent to a girls' mission and the New Testament took strange hold of her young fervid religious imagination.

"Mother," she said, "can you tell me—you who have four great sons— how I can bear a son?"

"What do you mean, little daughter?"

"Why, mother, I want to be another Miriam (the Virgin Mary) just as good as she; and have God for my son as she had. Can you tell me how to do this?"

My mother replied quietly, "If you meditate and are pure in heart until you grow up, God himself will tell you about it."

"I do hope He will not cheat me," my little sister sighed.

Mother fostered her religious instincts, but differently from mine, laying more emphasis on symbolism, as the Hindu custom is in the education of girls. For instance, one evening when we were at the temple listening to the recitation of the epics, the name of the wisdom god, Ganesa, was mentioned. My mother explained the symbolism of the god to her but not to me. Ganesa has four hands and my sister told me later that these four hands stood for the four Vedas. When God revealed the four Vedas He did it so fast that it took four hands to write them down. Whenever I wanted to know something about the gods, my sister could always tell me a story about them. She was trained to be a teller of tales, for "Woman must weave the tales around which man's life grows."

Manners also were an important part of her training. One day she ran across the room to speak to me and made rather a noise about it. My mother called her back, saying, "No daughter of my house brings misfortune by making her footsteps audible to others." When she took her turn with her older sisters in serving us food, she had to learn a certain grace of gesture. She was told to stoop, bending like a swan's neck; to sit down and rise silently like a fawn leaping in the dusk. She was taught to salute by putting her palms together and touching her forehead to them at the thumbs.

She learned by heart portions of the epics and the dramas, with particular emphasis laid on significant phrases. Once I lost a piece of silver. When I came home and told her, she quoted from the Upanishads: "We realize God by renouncing the things of this world."

A cousin of ours came to us after a long pilgrimage to Juggernaut. She talked continually about the riches of the pilgrims she had met and my sister said to me later, "Our cousin went to Juggernaut with a load of illusions, and has returned with her load still heavier. 'Whatever thought we carry, that is the destination we shall find,'" was her conclusion.

She was nearly twelve years old at this time. Every afternoon at four o'clock, after bathing and dressing for the evening, she used to put flowers in her hair and I had to find the flowers to bring her. But one day, when a mendicant monk was staying at our temple, she gave him fruits, although I had just brought in her afternoon flowers. I said to her, "Why don't you give him flowers?"

"I am a woman," she replied, "he is a monk. I cannot give him flowers, only fruit; because fruit has no sex."

One day I was swimming in the lotus pond to get flowers for my sister and I caught my feet in the stems of the lotus. I thought the water god was angry with me and was going to take me to his home, the moon palace, under the water. So I screamed and yelled for help and continually I felt the water god, pulling at my feet.

Suddenly this same monk appeared. "O thou brainless brother of a wonderful sister, why dost thou shout 'water god,' when it is nothing but lotus stems that have caught thy feet! Dive under water, open thine eyes and release thyself."

Choking and gasping though I was from the struggle, I managed to shout, "O pretender of holiness, dive thyself and open thine eyes under this muddy water if thou canst!"

He plunged in and rescued me and my flowers. But he would not let me bring the flowers home. He said, "I have touched them. Take them to the temple, not to a woman."

Once my sister and I were standing outside our front door when a strange man came and stopped before us. He had a cord around his neck and he began making a queer sound like the lowing of a cow. We spoke to him and he lowed again, continuing to make the same sounds in answer to all our questions. At last, much to our relief, our mother appeared upon the scene and we felt secure at once, for nothing ever frightened mother. She went about always unprotected wherever she wanted to go. Fear was not in her make-up. She looked now at our singular visitor out of her calm and steadfast eyes that never moved to the right or the left like those of some women, glancing this way and that in search of other eyes. She seemed to feel with her gaze rather than see, and she said to me, "Go fetch me my box of money." When I returned with it, she took out a piece of silver and gave it to the man, who bowed his thanks and departed.

We pestered her with our eager questions. "That man," she said, "has killed a cow by accident. Now he has put the cow's rope about his own neck and is going through the community begging for forgiveness. Everyone gives him a piece of money which is a sign of pardon. People forgive easily an accident of that sort, and he soon has enough to take to the priest, either to buy food for the people, or a new cow for the temple—generally the former as even a lame calf costs more than he can collect. In this way he expiates his sin."

"What happens," I asked, "if he kills a man by mistake instead of a cow?"

"He ought to be allowed to repent and be pardoned," said my mother.

"But he isn't, is he?" said I.

"No, but he ought to be," my mother insisted.

"I suppose it's different—killing a man"—this from my sister.

"Man, of course, believes so," said my mother, "but if you asked the question of the cow, what would be her answer, do you think?" But this was too much for our young heads.

My sister was taught many rituals, different from those I learned. One of these rituals was fasting. My father was opposed to this, but my mother said, "My lord, some day her husband may die, and as a widow she will neither eat nor drink for twenty-four hours every moon. Is it not better to practice fasting now, in case the hound of calamity leap upon her in the future?"

My father said, "There must be a change for the better in these customs. No widowed daughter of mine shall fast in my house."

And my sister answered, "O foolish father, if the life's light is gone, what matter how long one fasts?"

Widows are now allowed to marry by Hindu custom and yet as this practice was unknown for many centuries, most widows consider it too shameless even to be thought of. And when my eldest sister became a widow, she would not let my father mitigate any of the rigors of widowhood. My father, in spite of his principles, fasted with her, a not unusual practice. He did this out of love and sympathy. He used to say, "Since men have made such rigorous laws, it is good that a man should submit to them with a woman."

But my little sister was not to know in this incarnation either the glory of being a mother or the sorrow of widowhood. When she was about twelve years old, she fell ill one evening near sundown. It was the plague, and at dawn the next day her soul set forth again on its eternal vagrancy. My mother was taken ill that same night. I heard their delirious talk and firmly believed that they were conversing with God, because they were so soon to be with Him. How did I sense the nearness of death, I wonder? Did someone tell me of their peril? My mother recovered, but how long she was ill I cannot remember, nor any of the details of my sister's death. In India we live with death on more intimate and friendly terms than in the West, and it makes less impression upon us.

A Hindu woman's education initiates her into the primal wisdom of the race and trains her emotions through ritual. As my mother once remarked, "Woman must create friendship and love and must learn to face death, for she cannot give life without risking life. Thus woman's task is to sit between two deaths giving life through her breasts."

The peasant girls too have their training but it is less rigorous. We lived on the outskirts of the village, as I have said, and I used to wander in the fields at dawn, watching the maidens at their first morning rite, which was to gather flowers for their household shrines before which they burned a little incense to begin the day. I have often heard a young mother at dawn repeating to her baby:

"O my blessed child, raise your head! It is the hour of your worship; the sun has been lit in your temple. By giving you to the world, I may give a god to the world, therefore you are God-given to be nursed by me."

The country girls do not work very hard; indeed, their duties are more picturesque than arduous. They make garlands of flowers and put

DHAN GOPAL MUKERJI

them around the oxen before the men lead the beasts to the fields, and they milk the cows and sing the while:

As the milk sings into the pail,
The milkmaid's breast aches with the urge of motherhood.

They go about gathering flowers for the temple, and at half past nine there is the "parliament of women." In the houses thirty or forty women get together and gossip. The parliament is from half past nine to twelve o'clock. Then the heat comes and they have to sit still and meditate.

Their most interesting occupation is drawing designs on the walls of the house, usually lotuses and conch shells. The lotus is the symbol of spirits and the conch means speech of the gods. All over the walls are these mural decorations, and every three or four months they have to be changed. This decoration is the duty of the girls. Reading and writing they never learn. They learn numbers by putting seeds of some kind together and counting them. I have seen Indian girls trained by many foreign methods, but I have found our way to be the best for them.

In the afternoon they put on their prettiest clothes and visit each other and gossip. They give dramatic talks, and I have seen them do plays. In the evening, just before sundown, every girl goes to the river with her pitcher on her hip, her anklets jingling. And by the rhythm of the jingling anklets, you can tell whether the pitcher is full or not. Men make songs about it:

You go to fetch water in the dusk, which is tremulous with
the music of your anklets.
O, if I could, I would drown the dusk with the beat of my heart.

Later in the evening, the cattle come home with the men, weary after the day's work. This is called the cow-dust hour, because the cattle's feet bring the dust up in the air. The cow-dust, we say, is the cry of life to God, "How long, O Lord, how long?" The girls attend to the animals first. They give them to drink and lock them up. After the evening meal, the girls wait for the dusk to come, all sitting quietly. Then a very delicate thing, the consecration of the dusk, takes place. When twilight comes, they take a lamp in their hands and go softly around the house saying a prayer of consecration. In the evening they sit about and talk with their men folk. Then if there is a woman in the whole village who knows how, she will take down the Sacred Book and read it to the assembled men and women. Outside, the tiger may be walking by; within they will be discussing the question. . . "and the soul was never born, how can it condescend to die?" Outside the tiger is walking, but inside they talk of immortality!

One of the most vivid impressions of my childhood is associated with a little girl with whom my sisters and I used to play, and as it may throw some light on a certain Indian point of view, little understood by outsiders, I will set it down here, just as it impressed itself upon my young mind. This little girl was named Rangini. We did not know where she came from. At a certain time Rangini disappeared and I asked my sisters where she was, but they could tell me nothing. Then everybody forgot about her.

A long while after, when I was in the city for a few days with my uncle, I happened to see her late one evening standing at a balcony, and I at once knew what she was; she was a dancer, for it was a dancer's house. I stopped and she turned and went in without seeing me, and presently I saw her again inside dancing; her shadow was falling across the wall. She began to sing:

I came to fill my pitcher,
Why have you filled my heart?

She sang it, over and over, and it went through the open windows like a cry from the heart of Calcutta. I could vaguely see a throng of her admirers sitting in a circle around her on the floor. She danced toward them and swayed back; then sideways, and behind her on the porphyry wall her shadow trembled like a flame. One of the men was beating a drum, another playing an instrument with bells on its handle, which jingled in time with the bells on the girl's ankles, and with the throbbing of the drum. As she moved toward them, her flower-decked hair flicked their faces, and they sang: "What pleasure you give, O straying hair!" And Rangini sang:

I came to the black waters of the river to fill my pitcher and bring it home, but you stood in the way and now I go home; my pitcher is full, but my heart is empty. Who are you standing in the gloaming of the evening? I know you. You are the plunderer of hearts. Will you tell me which is the most beautiful heart you have stealthily garnered tonight?

Dancers are not necessarily prostitutes; the better the dancer, the more austere her life. The Indian understands perfectly to what grade these women belong—the professional dancers are usually nothing more than dancers. Of course there are prostitutes, but even to them is given an ideal of purity. Mr. Kipling makes a passing reference to this in his story *On the City Wall*. He says, "Lalun belonged to the most ancient profession in the world, and she was married to a tree who saw everything and said nothing." Those who know Hinduism from within can explain this.

When, after watching Rangini through the window that night, I returned to my home, I asked my grandfather to explain what I had seen. I said to him, "Has this girl been wedded?" My grandfather answered, "O thou curious beyond thy age, dost thou not know that even she has been wedded? No woman is denied that consecration, but certain women, friends of folly that they are, might fail when they attain their growth to remain true to marriage, and so they are wedded to a tree or to some inanimate object, whom they cannot betray. Their marriage remains an absolute vision of purity. Even to the lowest of the low the door of God must always be left open."

III

The Holy Man

The holy man, as we know him in India, is well presented by Kipling in *Kim*. The Indian holy man attains the simplicity of a child; the more childlike he is, the more holy. The holy man has a sense of humor; he is so holy that he has forgotten his holiness. This is the ideal of all Hindu life. To attain the spirit of childhood is the aim of Indian education.

I knew such a holy man. It was one of the great experiences of my life. I was about ten when I first met him. I do not know how he came to our village. He was a very peculiar person; he never ate more than one meal a day and he used to say, "If you know how to get nutrition out of food, one meal is sufficient." He never did miracles or tricks; people who came to him found him ignorant of the things they knew, but nevertheless they went away happy that they had seen him.

As a young man he had left the world suddenly, and wandered and wandered, and twelve years later he came back, because every twelve years a holy man is supposed to return and see his birthplace, and then go on wandering again. This is an old custom; I do not know its origin but every Indian feels the obligation; it is a law of the gods. My holy man came back to the village where his wife had been all this time, and took up his residence under a big tree near the house. He would go to see her in the morning saying, "I must go to the mother." This is according to the strange Indian belief that it takes two women to produce a holy man: his mother who gives him birth and his wife who, through meditation, consumates his spiritual birth.

He was a man of about forty, not very tall. When he arrived, the village went into ecstasies: "Our holy man has come!" When a holy man comes, there are torch processions and drum beating; it is an old saying that "wherever a holy man steps, there a new Benares springs into being." But there is also this saying, "no matter how great the procession, the time comes when the holy man has to eat his soup alone."

I came to him in the morning when the crowd had left and said to him, "You are alone now?" "Yes," was all he answered. He did not talk to me but I smelt his holiness as bees scent a flower.

Soon people from the neighboring villages seemed to know where he was. As it has been said: "The fragrance of the lotus goes with the wind, but the fragrance of holiness goes even against the wind." Wherever a holy man is, people will flock to him like swarms of bees, and they came mile after mile in caravans, on camels, on elephants and on foot, journeying six or seven days even, to see this man. They left presents, and he said, "They come to find in me what I search for in children," and he gave away all the presents.

One day he put his hand on my shoulder and said, "Little son, what are you going to do?"

I was nearly eleven. I said, "I don't know. What do you wish me to do?"

"What do you like to do?"

"I like to play."

"Can you play with the Lord?" I could not answer him but he said, "Do you know, if you could play with the Lord, perhaps it would be the biggest thing that has ever been done. Everybody takes Him so seriously that they make Him dull as death."

A large part of my life at this time, because I was the youngest son, was taken up in performing rituals—the marriage ceremonies and the burning of bodies. I had to give blessings to people whom I hated. Then this holy man came and said, "Away with rituals; go, play with the Lord!"

At another time my holy man said that if we could banish hate and fear, our souls would be holy, and since animals have souls, our souls could speak to theirs. He said, "The dumbness in the eyes of animals is more touching than the speech of man, and the dumbness in the speech of man is more agonizing than the dumbness in the eyes of animals."

Through all life is running the golden thread of consciousness which binds the world together—man, animals, stars. In the Upanishads and the Bhagavad-Gita God says:

I am the golden thread of continuity running through all. I am the seed eternal blossoming through all. I am the endless fire of truth stretching from planet to planet, from man to man, to the silence of the gods, and beyond them into my ultimate silence, which is the energy of repose.

We can recognize in all animals this fact of the unity of life. Young children in India are taken into the jungle to learn it. My holy man interpreted the jungle to us, saying, "The animals are our brothers.

They want to talk to us; we must understand them." This brother talk fascinated me because I understood nothing of it. He took two or three of us to the jungle at midnight, where each bough was hung with silence. One could feel the living jungle, a moving tide of being, but in a moment all was still. Nothing stirred. Every animal was frightened into immobility. We climbed into a tree, because our breath exhaled fear and hate, and kept the wild creatures away; but the holy man sat on the ground. In the moonlight we could see him, and presently the animals coming and going as if no one were there.

He used to play a flute in the forest and the deer would come and listen to him. The deer and the snakes are fond of flutes and perfume. Perfume hypnotizes them. He used to say that there is a power in sound that would put flowers to sleep if you knew how to play.

Once when I was alone with him in the jungle, he asked, "Are you afraid?"

"Yes, I am," I answered.

"I noticed it," said he; "you smell to me like a meat-eating animal, there is a stench of it. Put your back against a tree and sit still. Nothing can attack you from behind."

I did so. He too sat down and played an instrument which he had brought with him, and the song he sang went something like this:

> The moon is whispering into the shell of the jungle,
> She is gathering up the echoes of her own music.

Gradually I could see animals moving. And he said, "Are you still afraid?"

"No, not now." Perhaps it was the music that had quieted me.

He said, "Don't talk, listen!" And he whispered, "Do you sense the change of movement in the jungle? Now it is the homing hour; the feet of the animals are feeling for their lairs, and their steps are surer than when they are going forth at daybreak."

We sat through the night until the animals came out to bathe. "Now they are purified," said my holy man. "Feel them weaving dawn threads through the jungle! Their movements are like threads of stillness drawn from all directions!"

Then suddenly came a screech of gold in the sky and the garment of daybreak was complete. All the threads were woven in, and life was released to greet the morning.

That sense—how to greet the day—has been taught to the Hindu race by the animals. Life stands still for a moment and all the four-footed ones hesitate. The winged ones in the tree-tops give the word, and then comes the thunder crash of sunrise. Every blade of light is like a poniard stroke in your eyes. You seldom find a Hindu woman in bed after dawn. She is meditating; she has learned from the animals how to greet the day.

I came and told my mother all about that night's experience. She asked, "Do you want to follow this man?"

"I'd love to," said I.

But my mother shook her head, "Your time has not yet come."

After a while, my holy man visited our house. My mother saw him turning somersaults in the backyard to amuse the children and said to me, "He is indeed a holy man. You can follow him!" How did he know when to turn handsprings in order to convince a woman that he was holy?

At last the day came when he said, "It's time for me to go." All the village knew that our holy man was going. We all cried. He took me and five or six other boys with him, and we went about from village to village.

One day a very rich man came to him and said, "Are you the holy man?"

My master replied, "You know I have a pair of spectacles on my eyes; I don't see people as they really are, but only as they appear to me."

"How do I appear to you?" said the rich man.

"I see a goat's head made of gold on your shoulders," was the answer, and the man was very angry and went home.

A woman came for charms. "Why do you want charms?" the holy man asked.

"I want many children and all the wealth in the world," the woman said.

"I have no charms," he told her, "but I will tell you what to do. Adopt one of these boys and keep him in your house; he will bring you happiness."

"But I want my own child," she protested. Then the holy man said, "I cannot give you your own children. It is very well that you have no children, because you have desired a child so terribly that no child could live up to that desire."

One night we came to a rich man's house. Everybody bowed to us and gave us blessings and showed us every kindness, and boy-like I throve on it. To this house came a political agitator and made a speech. He said: "Since the British came to our country, many millions of people have died!" Then everyone was excited and the whole place was agog with rancor and terrible feeling, as he went on with this kind of talk. When he had finished, my master said, "I want to speak to the people, will you let me?"

"Yes, of course," the master of the house replied.

My master then arose and said: "This man has told you that millions have died in India as a result of British rule. For four thousand years spiritual immortality has been our heritage; how dare you bow your head to a Western myth called death?"

The crowd gathered around him and begged, "Tell us more!"

"There is nothing more to be said. Why don't you all look at each other and laugh?" he replied.

"What do you mean?" they asked.

"I cannot understand why you should create hatred amongst you, when you can be cured of this terrible distress by laughing at each other," was his answer.

Then the other man said, "You are nothing but a liar and a hypocrite and thief, and you have not the welfare of your country at heart!"

My holy man answered, "My friend, if you bring presents to a man and he does not accept them, what happens?"

"I take them home."

Then my master rejoined, "I do not accept your abusive words. Better take them home with you!"

Once a man who had been nursing in the cholera epidemic came to my master and said, "We have seen nothing but death. What do you make of it?"

"We don't really know," said my holy man. "You notice, of course, that there is a great deal of fuss made about being born and dying; but suppose we had been born and had died all at once? . . ." He was continually saying something of this kind: that our birth and our death had taken place at the same moment. "For example, a thing may happen in time," he said, "in the sixty years between birth and death; but in reality these sixty years have always been in existence. It is only in the material world that they seem to be passing by us." His point was that in reality we live and die at the same point of eternity. Later on this was confirmed by my mother's teaching, and later still, on the other side of the world, I heard learned men discuss something called Relativity, and although the terms were different, occasionally their ideas seemed to me very like my holy man's.

At another time he said a terrible and beautiful thing, "The urge of life is for happiness and yet when you find happiness you are mortally wounded." We were sitting under the tremendous boughs of the jungle that day. "See this vine which touches my forehead like a snake," he continued. "Early in the morning it hears the call of light and goes straight toward it. The same creeper comes back in the evening, burned black; it has been mortally wounded by the sun and lives only a few days. The tragedy of our climate is this urge for the sun; the tragedy of our people is that we have all heard the call of God, and having found Him, we are lost. It seems we are like the creeper; we want something so big that it kills us. Therefore, India disappoints. It is the land of the death god, Shiva. The dead live, and *they* are the reality of India. Shiva is alive because he is dead; he goes around India every three thousand years, riding on a bull, and he will go three times round; you smell Shiva's presence and continual death!"

Once my holy man took us to a neighboring city, where we stayed in a rich man's house, and in the evening many learned people came to see him. They discussed whether God was one or many, and of course they asked my master to take part in the discussion. He said, "God is one to those who have found Him one, and many to those who have found Him many."

One man was very bitter in his speech and I was quite curious about it. "Master, what's the matter with him?" said I.

"Don't you see," he answered, "the hunger for God is a genuine thing in the human heart. In his heart there is a tremendous emptiness. He is trying to fill it up with words; he is a sick man; no wonder he is bitter!"

They asked my holy man if he had seen God. He said, "Even if you touched God's hand, he would remain unknown. He is the origin that annihilates all origins; He is godless, that is why I call Him God. The moment you make Him a person He does not exist."

They said, "You are joking."

He answered, "Yes, God is the greatest Joke of the universe. Otherwise, why is it so many dull people are serious about Him?"

Once I said to my holy man, "I am so weak. What shall I do? Some people can reason God out. I know that God is the ultimate cause, but I cannot reason about Him; I am too much the victim of my emotions."

He said, "My son, your weakness should be the source of your strength. Emotion will lead you to imagination. Intensify your weakness so that it becomes your strength. Then you will find that it is nothing but a veil drawn over your strength. By intensifying your weakness you will break it."

Another time I asked him, "Why do good people suffer in this world?" He said, "Capacity attracts. When you pray for the rain you are also praying for the thunderbolt. When the tiger of calamity comes, may you not be found wanting!"

For a young boy it was all very hard to understand. I said to my master, "I cannot do all this." He answered, "Why do you try? You do not have to work so hard at it. You can reach God through your football. Play with God! He is the ultimate playmate of the world." He meant that all actions are related to the inner experience which is God.

His tongue was not dipped in honey; though his essential quality was compassion, he had no sense of charity. He did not want to impoverish one by his kindness, but to heighten one by his strength; he used to say, "Humble the Himalayas by being tall."

My fellow disciple was a great syllogizer. He always saw things clearly. I envied him but my master said, "That boy sees things so clearly that he is like a blind man in a dark room who will always find his way out, whereas the secret is to sit still in the darkness and let the Lord come and find you."

People began to seek him more and more, and they would sit around him and never speak, and suddenly one or two would break into tears and go home.

As I had my master, so had my mother hers. Although a Brahmin, he had renounced his caste, as all holy men do. But somehow his appearance betrayed his Brahmin origin. He could not help it. Though he wore the *Sanyasa* ochre-colored robe, he appeared to possess two superfluous yards of it which gave his walk a long flowing movement. His trident had three rings, to symbolize spirit, intellect and matter. Despite all this formality he used to play with us as my holy man did, and his favorite game was a sort of blind man's buff. He would blindfold all the children and would walk around stealthily like a cat, jingling his trident from time to time. The children always failed to catch him. At the end he would say, "Thus we perceive God here and there, but we can never reach Him."

We never knew when this monk was coming to our house. It was very strange, but he used to arrive whenever my mother was in trouble.

He always seemed to know it; no one knew how. He would suddenly appear and ask, "Where is my daughter?"

"My lord, she is in meditation."

He would say, "I will wait."

He played with us while waiting. Then he and my mother would have a conference; after that he would disappear again. He never asked for anything.

The last time I saw him was just as I was about to leave India. He said, "Your feet are itching for distance, but have you the power to destroy distance?"

I said, "How do you destroy distance, my lord?"

He answered, "By sitting still."

A man can travel with a great deal of freedom if he wears the yellow robe of a *Sanyasin,* and although all monks are not holy, they will sometimes wear the yellow robe in order to deceive people into thinking that they are. A monk, whether holy or not, will sometimes sit in your backyard without asking for anything, and without eating for three or four days.

Before a man becomes a Holy One he generally goes through a training of ten or twelve years. Then he has a spiritual experience or revelation which is looked upon in the light of a divine consecration, setting him apart by a sort of accolade of God from common men.

After some weeks of wandering with my holy man, I returned to my parents and my schooling. These sudden excursions in search of religion are a very common part of Indian life. It is the custom to leave the world at forty, take a begging bowl and go on a pilgrimage. Some never come home, others return in a short time. Both my parents left the world and traveled. When my mother went away, she was gone hardly three months before she came back. "The Lord is within me," she said, "why should I go all over India to find Him?"

My father said, "Everything is illusion." He kept on traveling for twenty years, but he never found the Lord.

"But why all this concern about God?" you ask. If the Lord exists, nothing matters. If the Lord does not exist, can anything matter? What are men good for if they may not become gods? Our fellowmen have become Christ and Buddha.

IV

Initiation

To every Indian comes his day of initiation. It is something like confirmation in the Christian church. Also the girls are initiated, though I do not know much about that.

Before my own time came, on one of my many journeyings, I saw in an isolated village of the hills the initiation of a carpenter. His mother brought the boy, after he had bathed in the river, to the family shrine where the altar fire was burning and the father and others of his caste were waiting. His father asked him first, "Do you wish to follow the vocation of our family?"

The boy replied, "Yes."

Then the priest asked him the same question. He took his oath: "I swear by the fire, by the elements, by my parents, by the deities, by the Living God, I will be a carpenter in order to create beauty and utility for man."

The father brought the old tools of the family and said to the boy, "These are your younger brothers. They want fulfillment and you, who have a soul, must help them. By using them to create beauty and utility for men, you will realise their destiny as well as your own."

The boy took the tools and vowed: "By the fire, by the elements, by my parents, by the deities, by the Living God, I will never prostitute these tools, but will use them to create beauty and utility for men." Thereupon, he went out to work, and first having been shown the oldest plows of the village, he set about to make one himself.

We Hindus look for no material solution of the problem of poverty. We have no devices for multiplying production. We think that we cannot change the situation mechanically, and that therefore we must solve it emotionally. So we make each man a poet, by consecrating him like a priest to his task, and this is the meaning of initiation. Industry is organized so that each man in his own trade, by working with his own tools, may release his creative spirit.

The time came when I was to become a priest. I was asked whether I wanted to be one. At the age of thirteen or fourteen to be a man and bless others is rather an alluring idea, so of course I said yes; I consented at once.

On the day of my initiation my mother took me to the river bank. We went out to where the dead were being cremated. The lights of the fires seemed to bite the shoulders of the Ganges. I said, "I don't like it."

"But remember there is no death!" she answered. "We throw off the body as man throws off worn-out garments for new ones. So does the soul rise out of the worn-out body."

I asked her, "Why do you tell me this?"

She replied, "How could I have given you life, if I could not explain death?"

After I had bathed in the Ganges, we went home together, and I went in to my initiation.

As we came into the room, my mother's hand in mine, I saw that the altar fire was lit. All the priests were there and the head priest and my father were standing together.

My mother said, "My lord, I have given him my last instructions. I have prepared him before he was born and after he was born. I consecrate him to you."

My father took me over to our family priest. He said, "I consecrate this boy to you because he wishes to learn the secret."

"Do you wish to learn the secret, my son?"

"Yes, my lord."

"Do you wish to learn the secret, my son?"

"Yes, my lord."

The family priest then took me over to the high priest. "Do you wish to learn the secret?"

"Yes, my lord."

"Has anyone urged you to learn the secret?"

"No, my lord."

"Have you any motive for which to learn the secret?"

"No, my lord."

"The boy is ready. Shave his head. Take him out."

They took me out, shaved my head, gave me an ochre-colored cloth to put on. I came in again. My mother was gone. Only the priests and my father were standing there. My father said, "You wish to take this vow?"

"Yes."

Then I went over with him; he and I stood on one side, the others on the other side of the altar. The high priest turned to my father.

"You have kept the vows of wedlock as you promised?"

"Yes, my lord."

"Do you consecrate the child in all purity?"

"Yes, my lord."

He turned to me, "And do you wish to be a Brahmin?"

"Yes, my lord."

"Do you know what a Brahmin is?"

"No, my lord."

"Only he who has seen God face to face or lives every moment in order to see God face to face, can be a Brahmin. Can you live that life?"

"I can, my lord."

"You swear by your father and your mother?"

"Yes, my lord."

"You swear by the elements and the fire, by the unknown gods?"

"Yes, my lord."

"You swear by the Living God you will keep this vow you are going to take?"

"Yes, my lord."

"What is your name?" I told him. "Have you a father and a mother on earth?"

"Yes, my lord."

"You have no more father and mother!"

"No, my lord."

"You have no relation to anyone any more!"

"No, my lord."

"You are standing all alone before the sacred fire, and from this time on the fire that will be given to you will be lonely, and you will be lonely with it. Are you ready to accept that loneliness?"

"Yes, my lord."

Then we sat around the fire. He took my hand and we meditated twenty minutes or more, and then I was told the most terrible thing of all.

"He is not on earth, nor in the water, nor in the sky, nor even in the father and the mother. He is the End ever sought but ever beyond reach. He is in you, in your parents, in every living creature; and being in everything, He is the most lonely. He is the Loneliness that is within you. He is that Terror whose beauty you must seek throughout the world, and He is that Beauty whose terror has kept the world away from Him. Therefore, carry this Terror within your heart, and go from door to door and say to each person, 'I stand like a mirror before you.

Have you your perfection to reflect in it?' And this is the aim of your life, to be a living mirror before every face that comes near you. Now swear by the fire, by the elements, by your father and mother, by the Living God; forswear all and go begging and be a mirror before the world!"

I took my vow. Then he said the last thing, "Your parents are dead. Your relatives are dead. You are dead. Only one thing remains—and that is your vagrancy for eternity. Go forth!"

As I was going out, my mother knelt on the threshold. She held my foot and would not let me proceed. "Go now, my lord, but come back to me! She who has taught you, lies at your feet to be taught again. Go gather wisdom—but you owe me wisdom before you give it to the world. Come back—there is another woman who must be a mother too. If you do not promise, I shall never let you go."

"Lady, your will is done."

She released me, and taking my begging bowl and staff, I went out.

So it was over. I had renounced the world and entered upon my two-year period of beggary. You cannot be a priest if you do not know how people live, and the best way to find out about people is to beg from them. So there is a law of the priesthood that before officiating in the temple, you must go begging from door to door. But at fourteen, to be turned loose in the world—even after forswearing it, makes one feel rather forlorn. I did not know where to go. So with the child's instinct still strong within me, I went back to my mother's house, knowing that here I would not be refused, and said, "Give alms to the beggar!" My mother came out with a bowl in her hands and said, "My lord, here is your rice." She bowed her face to the ground. Before that, every morning, we used to take the dust from her feet; this was the first time she had tried to take the dust from mine.

I went to the river's edge, made a fire with some charcoal and a few sticks and boiled the rice. I was about to eat it when a beggar came along and said, "Brother, I have nothing to eat." At fourteen there is a limit to unselfishness, yet I had to give him the rice and sit there and wait until he was satisfied before I could have any of it myself. I decided that it took even more than the tremendous words of the ceremonial through which I had just passed to enable one to abandon earthly considerations. Then I went to the river bank and wandered through the town and again sat by the river thinking.

I had often noticed the boats piled with fruit going down the river in the morning—heaps and heaps of all kinds of fruit, for India is given to the madness of much. This afternoon I saw the boats coming back, laden with grain. I saw the bare bodies of the oarsmen as they rowed, and the golden sunlight falling on their bodies. There were thirty or forty boats. The Ganges burned like tiger's eyes—fierce, tawny, strange. The men were singing as they rowed. It did not take me long to find out that they were singing one of Rabindranath Tagore's poems, and it was borne in upon my mind how complete was the union that exists between poet and people in India. Tagore has taken their songs and put unity into them. This is what the boatmen were singing:

> *The red clouds dance to lead us astray, and behind us*
> *is a mocking of dark.*
> *The sky quivers with its weight of gold at the water's edge,*
> *and we see you*
> *Smiling on the prow of our boat, O river goddess!*
> *Do not drown us in the night.*
> *If you must destroy us, let us be wrecked on the*
> *speeding wings of dawn.*

You cannot have poets if you do not have beggars. In India we have millions of beggars and they are always singing the poets' songs. I heard one of them now as the twilight fell:

In the vast blue the stars are lit, and the moon is in the midst, for the worship of Him who made them all. The forest brings its perfumes and the breezes shake the draperies of the trees. I miss the trumpet call to worship. But, O brother, listen to the cry of the human heart!

That night I went to the bazaar to sleep. When the beggars come at nine o'clock, it is a sign that the selling is over, and the game is up, and then the people tie up their goods. I heard two tradesmen talking.

"How has the day been?" said one.

"Considering how it began, it has not turned out ill," replied the other.

"It is not good to have a missionary open the bazaar with a Christian hymn."

"What did he say, brother?"

"He said, 'Come to the Durbar that Bibi Miriam's son has opened!'"

"Yes, I remember it all now," said the first, "poor Bibi Miriam, they crucify her son every morning in the bazaar!"

Then another merchant remarked, "Now that the beggars are coming, the trading is done; when beggars come to the bazaar, it is like vultures coming to the battlefield. The fighting is over. It is time to shut up shop and go home."

I approached and said, "Brother, give something to a poor man."

He said, "I will give you a copper piece. I had better do so lest you speak ill of me. Beggars have loose tongues."

The other merchant said, "It is wise to make money, but at the end of the day it is also wise to give something to a beggar, for who knows in the next world what may befall one?" All India is not spiritual.

I slept in the bazaar that night. In the morning I felt the constable's foot kicking me. "Little brother, it is time to go and bathe. The bazaar merchants are coming to buy and sell. Keep thy blessing for the midday; when they have made their profit, then they will give thee alms." As I was going to the river, a woman handed me a flower. "Take this flower. May you give forth holiness as this flower gives fragrance." When I came to the river, I had to beg for the first time among strangers, but strangers are the best people to beg from.

One thing I have noticed particularly, that when you beg you discover the extremes of human nature. People do not like beggars. They want to get rid of them, and in order to get rid of them, they give them a copper or a curse, and a curse is the easier gift to make.

Once I asked my mother, "Why so much begging? Why waste time wandering about?"

She replied, "I don't know why. But this is what I have heard: The Lord of the World, Shiva, who lives on the top tiers of the Himalayas, married King Duksha's daughter. The king never forgave this match, because his other daughters had married very rich gods and Shiva, being the Lord of the Universe, was destitute. In order to humiliate the newly-wedded pair, Duksha held a grand reception, to which all the gods and their wives were invited, except Shiva and his bride, Parbati. Parbati came, uninvited, and her father repeatedly insulted her in the presence of the company. He called Shiva naked like the sky, therefore shameless; a vagabond, always blowing his horn of silence to attract attention; a bringer of death, yet calling himself God of Immortality. These and many other humiliating speeches killed Parbati; she dropped dead. Shiva, who was meditating in the Himalayas, felt the mountain shaken to the roots and knew what had happened. He bounded from crest to crest, clearing the horns and shoulders of the hills. Suddenly, King Duksha saw Shiva's two arms lift up the dead Parbati and carry her back to the heights. The beggar God was Lord of the Universe. So a priest, to become like the god Shiva, begins and ends with begging."

V

PILGRIMAGE, BENARES

I had some sort of plan for my wanderings, and as I wanted to see Benares and the hills, I joined two or three other young priests who were going in that direction. We traveled by train to Benares. It is older than any other Indian living city today, at least six hundred years older than Rome, and it has no history. When I reached Benares, I realised that the very heart of India was there; I found stone upon stone telling of the ages that had gone before, but leaving the events unrecorded; I found the ruins of a Hindu temple many layers down, and on this a Mohammedan mosque and above this a Buddhist temple.

Properly speaking, India has no history. We as a race have no consciousness of it, for our history has been written mostly by foreigners—the Greeks, the Arabs and the Chinese. The consciousness of history as an asset of life and as an expression of our people, does not seem important to us. History is the record of man's relation to time, but the Hindu does not believe in time, and all our life, according to the Hindu's vision, is an illusion and something to be transcended. You do not write the history of a dream—you wake up from it. Perhaps this is hard for the Western mind to conceive, but after five thousand years of civilization, we had so much history that we lost interest in it. This world is an illusion of time and space, and to treat it as reality is another illusion; as the Hindu scripture says: "The blind will walk through blind alleys and will call these enlightened days. Such is the irony of being blind."

The Ganges flows through Benares. The walls of the houses lean over the river as though to hear from it some whispered secret of release from the burden of their mortality; many walls have gone down as the river eats away the earth. The Ganges, the Mother of India, is supposed to be very kind; but as I heard her at night, I felt as if a razor-sharp claw were tearing at the holy city. Like an oak tree falling suddenly Benares will go down some day. The river flows on—and these walls are leaning a little more forward into the water each year.

At night, when all the lights were lit, I saw on the house-tops people reading and reciting, and inside the houses more people singing, and in the stables still more people, singing and reciting. The whole place was charged with poetry; but below this flowed the sinister Ganges, the deep, ultimate Mother, and nothing will remain!

As I passed the stables, I heard a groom singing:

"I went to the sea and broke away the pearl, I went to the mine and wrung away the gems, but you do not smile. Tomorrow I shall go out and trap the very sun and throw him at your feet, then perhaps you will love me." This is what the common people in the streets were singing but on the house-tops the cultured were reading; they would read from the Sanskrit:

"There is only one truth, but there are four Vedas. There are only four Vedas but there are hundreds of commentaries. And no doctor of philosophy agrees with another, lest his egotism be hurt."

And again: "Truth is the bull of the universe, standing on the four legs of righteousness. He holds the stars together."

There were beggars too and there were the people. Beggars are not all priests by any means, for at one period or another of his life almost every man in India goes out to beg, and becomes a part of the indistinguishable throng. One of them sang:

"The night like a black panther walks by our door. O poet, the fierce word, the word you are seeking, is in the panther's mouth! Have you the courage to open it? And more than that, have you a heart fiercer than the panther's mouth, to give the word a more fitting home?"

Beauty in India always has a sinister quality. In Western art (the art of the last two thousand years) there is nothing sinister. It is beautiful and uplifting. But in the art of India there is a quality of fierceness; the formless is crouching in the heart of form. Here is another beggar's song:

"You are the beginning of the universe, because you are beginningless. You are the end, because no end can trap you. You are the source of all truth, and yet no truth can completely contain you. You are that terrible claw of silence which is burrowing under the house of man's words." And again: "Do not perform good deeds to entrap me. Do not speak of my perfection; I am not perfect. When you attain heaven, heaven will be nothing but a chain around your feet. For I am not heaven. . . You will find heaven only to loiter there as a drunkard loiters in a tavern."

These things are the beauty of Benares. In the morning I awakened to the sound of feet going, going, going. Then the sun rose, and I watched the life of the river. I saw the people all coming in their white and yellow robes and dipping themselves in the water. India is not sentimental: once in a while they do not cremate a body, and as I watched I saw a corpse float by. It was the body of a holy man who had just died. Holy men are not always cremated and as the bathers knew this, they were not disturbed. They descended into the flowing green-gold current and came out with the water dripping from them and glistening in the sunlight. Then they went up to the temples. Near the bathing place were the burning ghats and I saw the burning ceremony which I had often performed myself.

The dead body is gathered up on a pile of sandalwood; another pile of wood is put on top of that, and before setting fire to it certain rituals are performed by the nearest relative. The burden of the ritual falls either upon the highest or the lowest; if the oldest son is away the youngest takes his place. I, being the youngest son, had had to cremate many times. We used to go around the pile seven times and say this to the dead:

"O you who are now homeless on earth, homeless on the waters, homeless in the deep, do not seek the vesture of flesh again, but go! . . . Go where our ancestors have gone! . . . Take the path of silence where the sun wanders in quest of ultimate truth! Go, where the gods are waiting for you! Now you must blow the flute of silence, for death is purified by song."

Then you set fire to the pile, and when the fire is burning you must watch it six or seven hours. It is a curious fact that lean people burn longer than fat people, and fat people sometimes burn in four hours; it takes seven or eight hours for lean people to burn and even then the bones have not completely turned to ashes. When the body is consumed, the ashes are put into a pitcher of water. You bring your pitcher of water and break it and watch the ashes go down into the river: "Go down with the tawny Ganges into that turbulent being called the Sea." In Benares you see this ceremony continually.

The day moved on. At noon the intense heat was like a dragon stretched on the ground licking up the moisture from the earth—all the city literally cracked with dryness. Inside the houses they had palm leaves and fountains to cool the rooms, and there I heard the droning and praying of the people and the monks. Thus the afternoon advances, and at five o'clock life begins again.

In Benares you find yellow sandstone walls, and granite and marble interiors. The houses leaning to each other, hold together like people in terror. It is as if they knew that some day the Ganges will take them all away, and they want to protect themselves from this common danger.

As I walked about the city I saw women sitting fanned by their servants on the balconies of these houses. Pigeons walked about, gleaming and iridescent and here and there on the cornices were perched peacocks with spreading tails.

The owners of these beautiful creatures naturally wish to show them off to their friends, but how to keep a peacock at home in the afternoon has always been a problem. They usually leave the house in the morning and go hunting for snakes out in the country, and they do not come back again until night time. The peacock plays with the snake before killing it; I have sometimes seen it standing on the snake's body holding it in the middle, looking disdainfully down at the writhing creature. Suddenly the snake will make a stab at the peacock, thrusting its fangs out, and then you see a feather fly into the air; but the peacock has not been harmed, it is so thickly covered with feathers that the fangs have not touched its flesh at all. This surprises the snake very much and it makes another stab; but still the peacock stands there, as if to say, "Who is this fellow, trying to bite me?" The snake tries this four or five times, and the peacock will look at it in the manner of a scientific man studying a specimen; but in another moment the snake is torn in two, and the peacock sits down to its dinner. People who live in the country usually have a trained mongoose or a peacock about the house to protect them from the snakes.

To solve the problem of getting the peacock home, they have cultivated the drug habit in the bird. At a certain time of day the peacock is given a grain of opium: thus, no matter where it may be, when that time arrives it will come home begging for the opium. After the opium the peacocks will stay around the house and can be shown to visitors. The Eastern mind has found an easy way of bringing the birds home. In the West people would probably abolish the peacocks, exterminate the snakes and paint the cornices in many colors instead, or invent some similar device to take their place, but in India nobody will go to so much trouble. So people spend the afternoon in idleness. Once in a while a monk will come and sit with them.

The Indian house is built square, and it has designs painted on the walls of the rooms, and always a courtyard with a small pool or a fountain to keep the house cool. There is a place to eat, but not what could be called a separate dining room; we sit on the floor where the plates and the rice are served, and do not use forks. The majority of the people eat from banana leaves; as soon as the food is eaten, they throw the banana leaves outside and the sun scorches them so that they do not decay. There are many courses to our dinner and in most Indian houses the fire is never allowed to go out, and milk is kept boiling over it day and night, so that in the hot climate there shall always be a wholesome drink for the children. Near the place where we eat there are water and towels and soap. We wash our hands before we come in to eat and wash them again when we go out.

In the late afternoon I saw the walk of the young men of India, a panther-like walk. The men wore yellow togas, their swords were hanging by their sides; after them came elephants with gold caparisons, and servants carrying purple napkins, and there were miles and miles of this rhythmic walk of colors. Suddenly fell the black thunderbolt of night, the colors crashed and disappeared, and Benares, for a time, was shut within pounding walls of silence. Then the lights began to come out in the houses.

There is one place in Benares, famous throughout India, and little known to foreigners—little known to them because no Hindu can bring himself to speak of it to an alien, hardly even to another of his own race, so holy is it, so associated with the innermost experience of his soul. It is called the House of Peace, and for the reasons I have given it is impossible for me to do more than allude to it in passing, although some reference to it I must make in giving a faithful account of a Hindu's life. Kipling knew the place, but of course from the outside only. It appears in *Kim* as the house of the Tirthankars. Tirthankars means "noble spirits, the deathless grains of sanctity." People go there to meditate—rudderless souls drift down from all parts of India to Benares with the idea that in the House of Peace they may meet an unknown teacher who will reveal to them the meaning of life.

For some time I had not seen my holy man; I found him after I had been in Benares about a week; I asked him many questions and he said, "Go to the house of the Noble ones; sit there and meditate, and you will find someone to help you." At the age of fourteen it is impossible to sit still for four or five days at a time and I did not want to go very much. I had other places to see, but I went to the Tirthankars. My real problems were not very deep, so I invented imaginary ones. The teacher listened to me all day and then he said, "Will you meditate with me?" But that was work—I did not want to work at all, and I told him I had an appointment to meditate elsewhere. He said, "I see your heart is gay, and the head invents strange illusions, but play with illusions: you will find God through your play." So this holy place, where the burdens of many fierce hearts have been laid, opened its doors to a careless boy, and sent him forth again smiling, to his play.

VI

Pilgrimage, the Hills

After seeing Benares I started for the hills with a brother pilgrim. It took us nearly six months to reach our destination; each night we stopped and begged a lodging: sometimes we traveled with the caravans, sometimes with the strolling players. Once we met a company of players who needed someone to take the part of a monk, and the leader said to me, "You are a monk, a real one, why don't you come with us?" So I acted in their play. My business was to sit and listen to invocations and prayers. I had never before looked at an audience from the standpoint of an actor: it sat around us in a circle and we sat in a little cleared space in the center of the assembly. Whenever a character had to speak his lines he got up from the seated group and went forward, and after finishing he would come back and sit down among us. Women took the parts of women in this company, which gave it a somewhat disreputable character, this not being the custom in India. All the lines were said by the different members of the cast to the accompaniment of music, and whenever the sentences reached an intense climax of emotion, the speaker would suddenly burst forth into a song which was sometimes improvised on the spur of the moment. When the song was well known, the chorus of men and boys would get up and sing the refrain.

My company was acting a folk play, and the actors took a great deal of liberty with the text; it was half improvised. I remember one occasion when the play was going beautifully, the audience was tense with excitement, swaying in time with the song of the chorus. The hero and his enemy were bragging to each other, and the hero said, "I'll break your wings and throw you like a mountain into the sea; you will never rise again!"

The villain replied, "I will break your teeth and stuff your throat with them so that you can never speak again!"

"Then give battle!" shouted the hero, and drew his sword.

This was the cue for the chorus, who arose and began to sing in very sweet rhythm: "Don, O heroes, your gilded bravery," but the audience got up like one man and tried to stop them, yelling, "Silence, begetters of he-asses! we want to see his teeth broken and his throat stuffed!" And the chorus demurely sat down.

The day after this, we left the actors, and continued our way into the awful wilderness of the hills. The only place we could find to stop that night was in a temple. We were afraid to stay there, because we had been told that the temple was inhabited by supernatural beings. Pilgrims would feel ghostly hands groping about their beds at night pulling off their blankets. We saw nothing in the temple but a little idol, before whom offerings of fruit and flowers had been made. The little idol did not look very terrible, so we lay down; but we were frightened to death by night time as we waited to go to sleep, and expected every moment to have our blankets pulled off. As we lay in silence we suddenly heard singing, then a voice said: "I smell human beings here." Of course we thought it was one of the demons.

"My lord, we be monks, holy men!" we cried.

"What brings you here?" asked the voice.

"O, my lord, we had no other place to go."

Question and answer went quickly through the darkness, and as we clung together, a torch was lit and we saw that we had been talking with a mendicant monk.

"How do you come here?" We were too bewildered to answer. "Has anybody pulled your blanket yet?"

"No, my lord, not yet."

And plucking up our courage, we asked, "Why should our blankets be pulled?"

"I will tell you," said the monk. "A monkey sleeps in a tree near this temple; he steals the fruit that is offered to the idol, and at night he comes down looking for his food and pulls at the blankets of the pilgrims who sometimes sleep here. They think it is a ghost. The fruit I offer to the idol sustains the monkey's life."

"Why do you do this?" we asked.

"I think," said he, "that the monkey must have been a priest in the temple hundreds of years ago, and a bad priest: instead of looking towards holy matters, he used to fleece his people, and so when he was dead he was forced to be born in this form to expiate his sins and pay his *karmic* debt. The poor fellow stays in the tree and I feed him: I am tied up with him somehow."

We sat about the torch and discussed monkeys. "Monkeys are very amusing people," said our new friend. "You cannot leave money lying near a window when they are outside. Once I was careless enough to leave my purse on the window sill, and a monkey took it and ran up a tree with it. I returned and could not find it, so I went all the way to the bazaar and got piles and piles of bananas and put them under the tree where I thought the monkey was hiding. Sure enough, he saw them and finally threw down my purse; then he assembled the other monkeys together and they ate up all the fruit in no time!"

The monk told us another story: Once an Englishman killed a monkey near his house. All the other monkeys came around and sat in front of his house all day, as if there were a funeral inside. The monkeys wouldn't move. The Englishman thought they would kill him, but they sat still and mourned. In the evening they stole the monkey's corpse and dragged it to the place where the people cremate their dead, and there they left it, and finally men had to come down and cremate the monkey.

The mendicant asked us what we were doing.

We said, "We are Brahmins and this is our year of pilgrimage."

"Why do you want to be Brahmins?"

"Why not, my lord?"

"Can't you be more than Brahmins?"

"What is your meaning, my lord?"

The strange man replied, "Once I was a Brahmin but I was continually occupied with the ritual and had no time for God, so I renounced everything and disappeared. Now, I have all my time for God: for instance, I can take care of a monkey who needs me, instead of bothering with human beings!"

"Did you renounce caste?" we asked.

He said, "Yes, because caste stood in the way of my realizing God."

"But do you want to abolish caste altogether?"

And he answered, "No." Then he told us a story about the flexibility of caste in the early days.

"Visiva Mitra was a king who longed to be a Brahmin. Vasistaha, the head of the Brahmins, said to him, 'It cannot be.' The king replied, 'If you do not make me a Brahmin, I will kill one of your eight sons,' and the lad was killed. The next year the same thing happened and Visiva Mitra killed another of the Brahmin's sons. Four sons were killed and still Vasistaha would not give his consent, and at last the king threatened, 'I am going to kill your fifth son. Will you make me a Brahmin?' Vasistaha replied, 'No!' The king was about to kill the boy; then he stopped and said, 'What's the use of trying to be a Brahmin if you have to go to so much trouble?' And Vasistaha embraced him and said, 'You are a Brahmin now, because it has ceased to be of importance to you,' and the king became a Brahmin that day. The only way to abolish caste is to remove the desire even for the highest caste."

I will interrupt the story of my pilgrimage to explain a little about caste in India. The situation is a difficult one at present. The young people of the better classes want caste abolished: the common people do not want it abolished. A man in our lower classes may become wealthy and well educated, but if he wishes to live in India he will have to raise the level of culture in his own caste in order to be at home in it; if we abolished this system altogether it would result in his associating with the higher classes and deserting his own, which would remain unbenefited by his improvement. Under our caste system, a man who is born in the lower station and becomes rich, cannot get out by marrying someone above him; he stays in his place and does good to his community.

The caste system originated about four thousand years ago when the Aryan race came to India somewhere from Central Asia, the Caucasus or Norway, and settled in the foothills of the Himalayas in the valley of the Punjab. They settled in the same sort of snow-covered mountains that they had left behind. The word Arya is like the English word "daughter," which comes from the German "Tochter": the Indian word means "female son." In the early days the sons went to war and the female sons carried in the milk and made the butter. The word "daughter" means the one who milks the cows—and Arya means one who knows how to handle a plow and feed cattle. The people who settled in the valley were agricultural and raised cattle; those who lived in the mountains would come down when the harvests were ready and take the food away. The Aryans realized that they must protect themselves, so they formed the military class, called the warriors. The other two classes were automatically created—the business man and the politician, and the priest class. These three were the original Aryan castes. The military caste, however, which was created for protective purposes, became oppressive, and in one thousand years conquered the aborigines and instead of killing them made them into the servant caste.

These four castes go on to this day. We have no intermarriage; we do not eat certain foods together; rice, for instance, because rice is a liturgic food. A holy man ignores caste because he has passed beyond it; and in certain places, like Juggernaut, the City of the Lord, caste does not exist at all. A cobbler once came to my mother and said, "Will you eat with me?" And she did. I, being much surprised, asked her why she did it. She said, "My son, equality is an experience which is never false." We go to school with other castes, they come to our houses, but we do not eat rice together, or intermarry. If a person marries below his caste, he or she goes to the caste below. We may engage in any work whatever, it does not affect our caste. A priest has to be born in the Brahmin caste, but a monk, whether he belongs to the Brahmin caste or not, is higher than a priest, and if a monk comes into a temple, he occupies the first place because of his holiness. Though Vivekananda came from the lower classes, when he became a monk he was above them all.

The founders of caste were very astute aristocrats, who did not believe in equality. Whenever there was a rebel spirit in the lower classes, for him they provided a way of escape: the rebel could never become a Brahmin, but by his power of spirituality he could become a monk. It is a curious fact that Brahmins have very rarely attained God in our history. Always it has been the other classes who have attained Him. We Brahmins composed the sacred books, but most of the prophets and incarnations of God are from other classes. Buddha came from the warrior class: he meditated and became God. The only way to abolish caste would be to renounce the desire even for the highest caste.

To resume my story: The following morning we left the mendicant alone with his monkey. When we reached the next village there was nowhere for us to stay, so we went to the priest's house.

"O, holy priest, give us shelter!" we begged.

"Who are you?" he asked.

"We are monks," we replied.

But still he refused, "I cannot give you shelter."

"Why not?" we insisted, and this singular priest only growled, "All priests are like kites looking for offal. Can a kite feed a kite?" But at last he gave us permission to come into the basement of his temple. He was in reality a thief. At night he used to steal out and head a band of marauders; in the day he taught righteousness. "Brothers, trust one another," he would proclaim. "Be kind to one another. Don't lock your doors!" Then he and his band of thieves used to go at night to rob the places where his too trusting congregation had left their doors unlocked. One day during our stay in the village, he was caught red-handed. He denied his guilt and tried to accuse my fellow pilgrim of the theft, but no one believed him and he was finally handed over to the police.

I was once taken for something much worse than a thief, I was taken for an undertaker! Undertakers come from the lowest caste, and are despised because they live by exploiting sorrow. I was sitting at a burning ghat one day and the undertakers, after piling up wood and setting it on fire, went off to beat a drum and sing songs, while I sat and meditated upon the illusions of life. Suddenly I was roused by a man's sharp question. "Look here, undertaker, why don't you attend to your corpse?" he asked.

"What corpse?" said I.

At this he flew into a passion and cried out, "Art thou drunk? Dost thou not see the corpse that thou art burning?"

"That is not my corpse," I protested.

"Oh," he said, "I thought you were the undertaker. You certainly don't look too decent to be one!"

"That is because I have renounced the world," I answered him, rather pompously, I am afraid.

Then he became still more angry and began to swear at the undertakers, "O grandsons of thieves masquerading as undertakers, you have neglected my dead and left near it a little holy man who knows nothing!"

In the course of our journey we came to Brindaban, the holy place where Krishna is supposed to have lived. There are many turtles there that look like rocks crawling about, and when the monkeys are tired of jumping in the trees, they ride on the turtles and pretend to be men riding on elephants. No one is allowed to kill the animals in Brindaban. It is said that once Krishna wished to drink at Brindaban but had no goblet. He bent some leaves together and drank out of them. Since then, in honor to him, all the leaves have grown cup shaped.

All kinds of people come to Brindaban—holy men and rascals. If you go to a holy place in India you will find two kinds of people: the holiest and the most unholy. Holy men give salvation and unholy men take away your purse.

As Benares stands on the Ganges, Brindaban stands on the Jumna, which is the second holy river in India. These two rivers are called sisters, for they spring from the loins of the Himalayas. The Ganges is white and tawny, the Jumna is dark; originally she was white, but when Krishna left Brindaban, Jumna turned black with grief. In the evening, songs like these go through Brindaban:

DHAN GOPAL MUKERJI

O Krishna, O love-god, return to Brindaban;
Green evening stands still for your coming,
And the grief stricken Jumna is sorrow silenced.
When you come you may not know her.
She is black now, and lo, she has blackened the sea!

When we arrived it was late afternoon. The girls were going about freely, as is the custom there. They were singing, because human feet should always be accompanied by the breath of song, a hymn to Krishna:

O friend, I could not see Him well,
Only eyes unblinded of love, see the beloved well,
So He passed from cloud crest to cloud crest;
And as the cloud heart breaks, so is my heart broken,
But it cannot shed its love.

And then they sang:

I went to the well to fill my pitcher;
Why dost thou fill my heart?

The town constable was going his rounds. When he met the girls, he sang:

You have taken my heart in the net of your eyes;
Do not send me away, O fatal fowler,
I seek to give you my sorrow too.

He sang this to chaff them, and the girls cried, "O constable, wake up. The thief will steal your lantern." He went his way singing. The constables do not protect the people, and once I remember when a thief attacked us the constable hid with us, saying, "Why should I risk my life for seven rupees a month?" A constable has no pockets but this one had a turban which was nothing but a pile of silver.

I asked him "Why do you carry silver in your hair?"

"It helps to keep the turban straight," he replied.

We reached the hills at last, just at dusk. The darkness fell like waters of silence, and the peaks disappeared. A raven flew by, and his wing-beat scratched the silence until it almost bled with the sound. For a long time there was not a single light visible in the valleys and no star dared put out its silver foot. Then came the call of the moon-bird, and silence walked away, giving place to the night sounds. You could feel animals' feet moving through the far spaces, and lights from the villages looked like tiger's eyes, and suddenly, as we looked up, all the stars leaped at us.

We slept and were up long before sunrise. As the blackness of night broke, the sun rose over the tops of the mountains. It was as if an eagle of gold smote the heavens and tore asunder the thunder-throated clouds, while below the fierce peaks opened like the petals of a lotus. I realized the meaning of the words "The lotus is the jewel of the spirit." The Himalayas had been closed in darkness and then the Sun seemed to unfold them.

Toward midday we came to where the Himalayas began to tell us everything: we heard the booming of the cataracts falling from far up in the rocks, and the little rivers screeching, the moan of the tiger, and the screaming of the eagle, while above all, the vast white head of the mountains rose saying, "Nothing matters. Sit still. I have sat still thousands of years, and because I sit still the rivers flow, the eagles fly and the tigers call." Then for the first time I understood what was meant by silence and being. My holy man had said:

"By sitting still, you have the world between your two feet; by lying down, you are present at all points of the universe. It is swifter than the swiftest flight of man's mind, this My being, because I am stiller than the mountains. Find Me in the very silence of your own heart, where I sit."

As we went on, I remembered the story of the fawn: At a certain time of the year, the fawn begins to smell musk. It runs through the forest in search of this musk, but never finds it. At last it falls down exhausted, and in its agony it licks its own body, and there it finds that the musk is growing. I had been told, "Do not be like the fawn, perishing in search of the musk in the wilderness without. Look within and find Me there, because I am your Infinite Self, waiting to be discovered. Find Me within you, and you will find the world filled with Me."

When at nightfall the darkness came upon the Himalayas, again the same thing happened. It was very extraordinary. The stillness began to rise, and the stillness was like ink, and the light began to recede from peak to peak, and this monster inkiness rose up almost to the very top, and the highest peak stood out alone.

You know stillness is not silence; it is absence of sound. Beyond stillness is silence. Sometimes when you hear the approach of silence, it is like the breaking of the ear drums. In the presence of the Himalayas at twilight we felt the pounding of silence like something crashing, and then it was gone and night descended. The animals began to move and we heard their night calls.

If there were no mountains there would be no Hindu philosophy. Below the conscious self of man is the world of unconsciousness, of real being. That is what the mountains have taught my people. This day of my pilgrimage showed me the depths of man's spirit. The seeker after truth is driven back and forth from the multitude to solitude, finding in solitude the truth by which to test the multitude; and when that fails, finding in the multitude the truth by which to test the solitude. Go to the jungle to find the silence of nature; then go back to human beings where there are deeper silences of which nature can never speak!

"I am beyond speech and thought. . . I am the Ultimate Silence. Over Me gathers the dust of sound."

The Cashmere Shawl

In the hills I saw the making of a Cashmere shawl. In olden times, as nowadays in the remote villages, men used to weave muslin by hand and go to the bazaars to sell it. A weaver would plan his work, put it on the loom, and as the loom hummed like a musical instrument the man would become taut, eager. Towards the end, his body would almost break, as the loom went on and on, until at last the muslin was finished. Then he would sell it, calling it by a name—"Morning Dew" or "Evening Silence." Even now, families two or three hundred years old have names for their clothes; you will hear the daughter say she is going to wear "Evening Glow," or the boy will wear "Noon-day Ease," and so on.

But the making of a fine Cashmere shawl is a greater thing than the weaving of a piece of muslin. About twenty men sit around the loom, journeymen and apprentices; it is like an orchestra. They all have a vision of the design, but the master who has done it hundreds of times to the minutest detail, he alone knows it. One holds the red, another the blue, another the russet, the green, the purple, and so on; all these threads are held like tongues of flame. The master has a small cane in his hand; he says a short prayer and the weaving begins, first the red, then the green, then the purple, and they begin to sing:

What are you weaving? We are weaving the little garment of a child. What are you weaving? We are making the dress of a bride. What are you weaving? We are making the chaplet of the dead.

So the whole gamut of life is sung.

Day in and day out this goes on. The master touches this weaver and then that one with the stick, and each responds. You begin to see the colors coming out, as if someone had torn the sun into ribbons and was weaving it into the pattern, and gradually this flow of colors takes shape and form. The work lasts about twenty days, and at the last the body of each one of these men becomes taut, like a full-stretched bow; the master stands like an eagle circling over his prey, the threads are a thunderstorm of colors—the weavers give a terrific yell! The thing is done! Then you see a marvelous Cashmere shawl. And they give it a name: "The True," "The Well-Made," "The Pride of the Maker," or "The Pride of the Possessor." It is ready, then, for the market. Anyone who has seen the terrific bow-like stretch of the bodies of the weavers towards the end of the weaving can never forget it.

I have seen the traders come mile after mile to obtain these shawls. Once when a tradesman from a European country saw one in the making, he insisted that it was only a mechanical process, a work of habit, and he talked about it so much that in that village the weavers became conscious of the design. The secret was lost to the village because the merchant had made the weavers think about what they were doing and they became entangled in the inhibitions of self-consciousness. Even in the artisan's work he must proceed from instinct to consciousness and from consciousness to unconsciousness. All his life the artisan has been taught to work unconsciously, in order to attain perfection, and the whole effort of the Hindu race is directed toward the attainment of this unconscious wisdom.

I saw the native potters at work in the mountains. The Japanese and the Chinese clay is carefully selected and is excellent, but the Indian is indifferent to the quality of his clay. A potter will take any mud and go to work on it, but while the material is imperfect, the form of his vase will be perfect. We rose early one morning and found a potter sitting waiting for the sun to rise, and as the sun rose he went to work, and the clay looked like a little mountain in the middle of the wheel. He put his finger on the clay and as the chalice was forming, he sang:

My heart, do not be like the wheel, but be like the center of the wheel, which is standing still. The wheel whirls because the center of the wheel is still.

A potter gives beautiful names to his wares, "The Nest of Milk," or "The Homing Place of Honey." When he is selling them he asks, "What will you have? Three Homing Places of Honey, or Three Nests of Milk?"

We stayed near this potter a long time. He said he could make any kind of pot or vase, provided people gave him the order and never came to ask him how he was making it. We wanted to put many questions to him but he said, "You should never disturb a maker by asking him how he makes a thing; he is like God, too busy creating to answer questions." If a potter becomes conscious of the process he loses sight of the thing itself. He said, "It is not the clay and the shape of the cup that is the most important; it is the hollow that holds the milk that is important, and you must know how to make the right hollow, or you will not be a good potter."

When we came down from the hills to go home my friend left me to take another way. I came all alone to a village and sat near a little river, meditating, when a woman passed me and said, "Son, you have a sweet face. Why are you here? How have they the heart to turn such a boy out into the world?" She took me home and gave me food; then her husband carried me to the next village in his ox cart. These villages are nothing but human dots on the edge of a vast forest: we have never cut down our forests any more than is necessary, since the animals are our brothers, and nature is a mirror of humanity.

As the farmer drove me along, I asked him about a certain holy man whose fame had reached us. His name was Pahari Baba.

I said, "Did not he live here once?"

And the farmer answered, "Yes; he used to live on yonder hill, in a cave. Ah! Since he died, our village has not been the same at all."

"Why is that?" I asked.

To which he responded, "Perhaps you have heard that as long as he lived, the Holy One did nothing for us and the villagers complained. We used to bring him rice and leave it at the cave's mouth; he took our gifts, without even a blessing. Presently he died, and very soon after that, a crime occurred in the village, a murder. The five elders of the village sat together and contemplated the bloody deed. One of them said, 'These thirty years the saint lived on yonder hill, and no crime occurred amongst us. Now that he is dead we are beset with evil, there is no one to transmute it.' 'Yes,' the others said, 'by his very being he overcame the forces of destruction.'"

In the next village as I was looking for shelter I found a peasant tilling the soil, and a Christian missionary talking to him and telling him that our God was different from his God. I was very tired and I sat down near them. At eleven o'clock the man stopped his work to rest for the hot hours. The missionary, bidding him goodbye, said, "Now you understand, there is a difference between the false God and the true God."

The peasant answered, "You are an educated man, and you see the difference; but I, being ignorant, feel that God is one. Of Him we have been given several descriptions, that is all."

Throughout India there is this primary wisdom of the common people. That night about ten o'clock I asked a common man, "Brother, what is happening?"

He looked up and replied, "The moon is gathering sheaves of silence in her arms."

Many things might be told about the rich well of Indian life, but there are three hundred million people in India and what I know is but a cupful.

Before sunrise I went to bathe. The people were taking the water of the river and touching their foreheads with it three times; this signified a prayer: "O mother, I am going to give you my impurity, but as you bathe my body, also wash the impurity of my inner life." This starts the day. After bathing, they put a mark on their foreheads with ashes, or dust or sand, to signify that the truth cannot be found with the blindness of two eyes, but by opening the third, the inner eye. When the sun rises he is the third eye, he is the messenger. The common, average people that stay on the soil are continually thinking of the Lord.

On my way home I stopped to rest beside the door of a Mohammedan butcher. He sold meat to the Mohammedans and the Christians. I sat down and he said, "What do you want here?"

"I am meditating on God," I answered.

"It's time for me to pray, too," he said; "I am a Mohammedan, I ought to pray; Mohammedans are better than Hindus."

"Yes, I've heard that before," said I.

"But I never pray," he went on.

I was startled: "Why don't you?" I asked.

He said, "How can I? A cow is larger than a human being and if you kill a cow, you can kill a human being. I live by killing, and so I cannot pray to Allah; yet if I can get to Him at all it must be through my killing."

I said, "You are just like our people."

"No, no," he answered me, "Hindus are infidels. They are no good; but I do think it is terrible to kill a cow! We do not kill our mothers because they give us suck, but after we have taken suck from the cow, we kill her!"

If I did not find a lesson in one town, I went on to the next, always searching for an experience of the inner life.

VIII

Idols

Before I returned to the duties of the priesthood which awaited me at home, I visited some of the great cave-temples of India. The importance of Hindu art, like the importance of Hindu life, lies in the background of its religious significance. Our art is extremely symbolic; there is a deliberate endeavor to make it ugly and so wherever you go in India you will find that all the beautiful things are marred by symbols. Beauty, is not enough. Beauty is poor fare for anyone to live on, and we destroy it where we can by the brand of holiness.

Children are taught: "We have goodness in one hand and truth in the other, but we have holiness within us. We go from beauty into goodness, and from goodness into truth, and from truth into holiness!" These are the four stages of man's life. All beauty should be marred by truth so that man can never escape from that fierce enigma of enlightenment which lies behind the appearance of beauty. This is shown in the celebration of Kali which takes place every year, in the autumn when we make the image of the Mother of the Universe—the image of Kali. Kali is the goddess of Time. She is dancing, because as Time is a succession of moments, so is dancing a succession of movements, and the only way in which art can express time is as a succession of movements.

Kali wears a garland of human heads around her neck, and she has four hands to symbolize the past, the present and the future. The first two hands, holding a sword and a human head, represent the present; man, the latest embodiment of human destiny, wiped out by death. The next two hands give the conventional gestures to indicate hope (the future) and memory (the past). Kali is shown stepping on Shiva, the snow-white god under her foot, the embodiment of eternal renunciation, whom she cannot vanquish. Her movements are arrested, for Shiva is unconquerable by Time. You tell a child to say to Kali, "O Mother, take away the vessel of Time! Show me the humble face, the face of thy silence, of thy love which has been hidden away by the dance of Time!" And to Shiva, "Lead me from the unreal to the real, from darkness into light, from death into immortality! O thou face of terrible beauty, penetrate me through and through by thy compassionate disillusion!"

DHAN GOPAL MUKERJI

When we make the Mother in the autumn, we get the clay from the heart of the Ganges; the whole town follows in the procession and it is a great occasion. I remember going once with my grandfather. The procession stopped before the House of Ill Fame and took the dust from the door of the house and mixed it with the sacred clay, and I asked, being still something of the curious child, "Why do we this?" "Don't you see," answered my grandfather, "we make the image of the Mother, and it is not complete until all motherhood is included in it. This is motherhood utterly ruined, but even those who dwell here must be reminded that they hold imprisoned something greater than themselves, and this is the way to remind them, for without their heart the Mother's heart is not complete."

Then we came to the house of Vaskan, the sculptor. We call a sculptor the sunmaker, for he puts light behind appearance, and rouses the sun of form in the formless. Vaskan received the clay given to him by the priest and all the people; then we turned away and left him, for in order to be prepared to make the sacred image, Vaskan had to fast and to meditate. When the image was completed, the priest, accompanied by all the village as before, returned to Vaskan's house and we found that he had represented Kali in one of her incarnations, as Durga, a ten-handed goddess. This image of Durga, who was Kali, stood on a raging lion who, in turn, stood on a slain buffalo. Motherhood is first a beast of burden, hence the buffalo; next a beast of conquest, hence the lion. Durga is ten-handed because she is the mother of the universe, armed at all points by her sanctity.

When we were gazing at the statue, the priest invoked the spirit of motherhood to dwell within the idol. He said: "O spirit that is formless, come and embrace this form so that we can worship by visualizing you through this appearance. O you, that dwell in all things as the Mother, we bow to you!" Then the procession carried the image to the temple, and for three days ceremonies were performed before it, including three miracle plays. At the end of this time, the image was again carried in procession and thrown into the river.

That evening people called on each other, irrespective of caste or creed, with the greeting: "Brother, we are motherless today, partake of this refreshment!" This was a symbolic communion, and on leaving they embraced each other, with the feeling that they had been initiated into brotherly love through these three days' worship. Now that the symbol had been destroyed in the river, the disembodied soul of motherhood became all the more powerful, for the form had been cast aside that the spirit might be retained. So the highest reach of art is to annihilate art.

According to the Shilpa Sastra, in which the symbolic art of India has been thoroughly explained, certain rules have been laid down for the guidance of artists. One of these is that the novice should not be taught the technique for the asking. He must meditate, and find within himself a vision that clamors for expression, and only then may his masters instruct him in technique.

In India all our art is ritualistic, especially the art of the temples and the caves. When I went to the cave temples, to Elephanta or Ellora, I found mountains hollowed out, and temples built underneath them. The columns supporting the roof resembled elephant legs, and the ceilings and the walls were gorgeously decorated with the sculptured forms of human beings and of gods.

About 200 B.C., or earlier, a group of monks went to meditate under the rock of Ajanta. In their meditations they experienced ecstasy, and having experienced it, they carved it on the wall. The monks who came after them began to dig in for more space, and built more shrines for the particular visions that they saw, and in the course of time they covered one side and then another of the mountain and gradually built entire valhailas there. The story of all the gods of India is carved on these walls, and the youngest of them all is Buddha: he is a young boy, compared to Shiva, Vishnu and Brahma. Seven hundred years of Indian history is written out in these caves, covering vastness with terrific forms.

I shall never forget my first visit to Ellora, reached after a two days' tramp from the nearest town. When the sages of southern India wanted to create an image of the universe, they went to Ellora. They worked for one hundred and fifty years and used up generations of artists. They carved a mountain into galleries, and as these rose higher and higher, they gradually attained the summit, and the whole mountain was covered, as the Himalayas are covered, with strange life. First, there are stone lines like serpents running around the base, miles of them, interlacing themselves, swallowing their own tails; these symbolize time, the time process. Then come elephants and lions, above them a whole story of men; then come the demigods, with their strange faces; then the supernatural, the ultimate gods, and at the top shrine is the sanctuary of silence: four bare walls. It is in this chamber that the supreme ecstasy was vouchsafed to man.

As I walked in the dim light of these galleries, faces of gods and beasts flashed into life and filled the air with strange presences. The pythons running in and out seemed more sinister than real snakes, peering faces of animals and demigods gave me the impression of a distorted jungle turned to stone. Then I came out by a small tranquil pool where sat a little statue of Buddha meditating. Here was the link between man and the fierce gods. Here was Man-God, God-Man, that which man can become. The statue sat as if to tell us that perhaps out of man's meditation the Heavenly City might appear. Man is the fulness of the universe; in him is enclosed the secret; within him lies this vast world of pythons, gods and the One God. If some man like Buddha comes again and meditates, perhaps the Heavenly City may return, more real than all these stony presences now shrouded in darkness.

In the cave-temples, after a labyrinth of rooms filled with saintly presences, I came upon an empty chamber. First I had passed through the beauty of the symbolized world and from that I had entered into this inner world of silence, and as I sat and meditated, I gradually heard and saw and felt the silence falling down the walls. That empty room was the key to the meaning of the entire scheme of sculpture.

In India throughout the ages, the nature of the human and the supernatural have interlaced, there has been no beginning. We have no prejudice against the lower animals, and the gods have no prejudice against us; the three go together with never a break. Though nature is implicit in God, it is continually becoming explicit in the world, and we think that the purpose of art is to release the impetus of nature through symbolizing appearances; as the purpose of philosophy is to release each man's sense of truth; as the purpose of religion is to release each man's spirituality. In every branch of Indian activity it is taught that a man owes no obedience to any master until he has felt this obligation first within himself.

We are continually testing the infinite in terms of this world, for if civilization did not have the infinite, the finite would break down. The whole culture of India including its art seeks not to reform the finite, but to inform it with the infinite. If you do not create God out of your own imagination, God will not be able to create the universe. God is the Tiger of Silence imprisoned within you; bring Him out to destroy the insolence of words!

"I am waiting for my ultimate utterance. Let Me loose! I want to wipe away the impurities of life by supreme rebellion. I am the River of Sanctities. Why do you lock me up within and bathe in the rivers of earth? Unlock Me and let Me out to purify the world! Uncage Me, the Infinite!"

IX

The Priest

My time of pilgrimage was over, and when I came home I took up the life of a priest.

The priest begins the day by opening the temple. He blows the conch, opens the doors, and people come and sit in silence for a few minutes. Religion in India, as in every other country, is kept up by women, and all the women of the community come in the early morning and sit still in the temple. The priest has to sit still with them to set the example of quiet, and that is hard work!

At seven o'clock the children bring flowers with which he decorates the temple, then he goes downstairs and into the kitchen, where there are many servants waiting. After consulting a clerk he gives them the orders for the day: "I think we may expect fifty poor people by noon, so prepare dinner for fifty." There is an income for this charity, as all temples are endowed, and the clerk keeps the account if the temple is a large one, otherwise the priest does. The temple remains open all the time and the people come and go and the children play on the stairs.

At nine o'clock the priest begins to read. He takes down the scriptures and reads purely for his own edification; people come and sit there and ask him questions, but there is no sermon; then, about ten o'clock or so, when he finishes reading, he goes around the countryside to see what has happened to the people. When there is sickness, it is his job or his wife's or his children's to act as nurse, for he is nurse, teacher, servant and holy man to them all. After going his rounds, he returns to the temple. The food is now ready and the priest, after a brief meditation with the people who have come in from the outer court, consecrates the food. During the afternoon everybody is asleep or meditating. In the basement, under the trees and all about, the people sleep.

The temple opens again at three or four. Then begins the hour of social intercourse when the villagers come in and sit about and talk. In India the gods are not disturbed by this sort of thing! At five a bell is rung and the end of the social hour has come; there is no cooking after that; no lights are lighted, the people wait in silence for the darkness. The priest has to meditate with them and when the hour of silence has passed, he blows his conch shell and then takes up the epics to read. All the laborers from all around, high and low, come in the evening to listen to the epics; after six or eight years of this they know them by heart—instead of reading the newspapers our people read the epics. In a village, about three quarters of the people come to the temple, which is to them what post office, town hall, community centre, and church represent in a place of similar size in America; in a town, only about a third of the people come.

Every temple is a theatre, as it used to be in Europe in the middle ages. The priest must give thirteen plays in twelve months. He has to select strolling players as they happen to pass through the town for these performances, which are more or less derived from the epics. The plays are free to all and sometimes two thousand people will come to see them. The temple pays the players, for a special fund from the endowment is set aside for that purpose. When a play is over, the priest says, "O assembled people, do not talk: go home and meditate and make it part of yourselves!"

The priest has to do all this; but it is merely routine work. Although he seems to be occupied with holy things, in reality he has no time for God. His duty is that malicious thing, doing good, which is enough to dry up anybody. Very few priests recognize that God has a sense of humor; that is why most of them continue to be priests. Half of them never do anything but sit down to this routine: they are spiritual vultures. But now and then one of them, when he is about forty, renounces the world and goes away from it all.

When a holy man comes, the priests give the temple up to him. My holy man used to come to our temple once in a while. He had charge of all the rituals at this time and he would simplify them very much. He would not read from the holy books but would sit and tell tales and chant and praise God. He said, "Praise when you come to God. Praise is the only way of defining God."

Nobody addresses the people except the priests and the holy men, but once in a while a master who is a scholar is invited. He explains the symbolism of rituals and speaks for five or six evenings on the sacred books and then goes away. Thus the epics are kept alive.

In India everyone is taught through symbols; therefore we make idols, each one symbolizing something, and through these we educate the people. If your prayers are personal and you wish to ask for something for yourself, you address the idols. You pray to them for everything you want, though they never answer your prayers. I asked my master once, "What is wrong with prayers?" He said, "Praying is a splendid thing; but everything that I ever prayed for, if it had been given to me, would have proved a calamity. We ought to say, 'O Lord, hear me pray but do not grant my prayers!'" In India we pray to the idols, but to the ultimate God, never. Idols are the impersonation of our desires which are both released and satisfied through prayer: a prayer to an idol is like confessing to a deaf and dumb person. We dare not insult the real God by asking Him for things.

I remember once an English lady came to see my father. In our courtyard she passed a man sitting before a little stone and praying his head off, and this English lady said, "How superstitious!" When he had finished praying, the man's face was illuminated; he looked up and said, "Madam, if a stick or a stone reveals God to me, how dare you despise it?" Idols are symbolic manifestations; we make them ourselves and to us they symbolize the temporary God. Every house has an idol and every evening the people sit still around it. They make a figure of clay or pick up a stone and say, "O spirit, come and abide in this!" and whenever they wish, they get rid of it. Although the common people become attached to their idols and grow very superstitious, if you ask them why they bow to them they will answer, "It is not the idol we bow to, but the spirit we have invoked and put into it." Even the simplest people will answer in this way.

In the Brahmin caste both men and women may become priests. Usually when the man of the family is dead, the woman becomes the priest. My sister is running our temple now and it is run more efficiently than when we men were there. This temple has been in our family for many hundred years. It is an enormous place with an estate attached, and my sister collects the rent and spends it on taking care of the poor. She is in charge of all the activities of the temple and takes nothing for herself except two meals a day. About twice a month she fasts for twenty-four hours. In our temple two priests are enough: sometimes there is one priest and an acolyte, but in a large temple like the one at Juggernaut there are as many as fifty priests. The Brahmin priesthood is not organized in the Western way and this gives it the advantage of flexibility. You can be a Brahmin without being a priest: you become a priest if you wish, and if you wish, you are allowed to resign, but you are still a Brahmin. Two-thirds of the Brahmins are not priests but lawyers and professional men; they cannot intermarry with other castes; and as they are not priests, they cannot go into the holy of holies in a temple.

　　　　　　　　　　　　　　DHAN GOPAL MUKERJI

When I came back from my pilgrimage I went into the temple, as I have said, and did this routine work. I used to marry young people, take care of the sick and read the epics. Besides performing all these duties, while I was running the temple, I went to the Christian school, and studied the New Testament carefully. It was hardly a year before I gave up being a priest, because I realized that I was not in my right place.

This may seem very strange to a Westerner after all I had experienced, but to a Hindu it was not strange. A Brahmin boy often fulfills the duties of a priest for a time, but if he finds it is not his vocation he is expected to resign and to seek the Lord in other ways. We think the end is holiness, not a profession. I was very young—hardly sixteen—and I was impelled by an urge which I did not myself fully understand at the time. All I knew was, that after seeing the vast spaces of India, I could not stick to my school, nor could I see myself continuing to sit in a temple giving blessings to people who could do without them. What I should have done perhaps was to have become a monk; religion did not spell priesthood to me and it never has, it is a call of the soul to go in search of that Vagrant of Eternity whom we call God. Distance summoned me. The Himalayas with their upward gesture and hunger for Heaven carried me away. No temple spire was tall enough to take the place of the *Dorj*, the home of the thunder, and *Sumeroo Himadri*, white heaving of the hills; and I could go, I was free, thanks to the traditions of a race accustomed in child, in boy, in man, to the restlessness for God.

X

Trading Shawls

Before leaving home again, however, I determined to go on studying for a time and to see what knowledge would do for me. But I only confused myself. I could not find contentment and I soon made up my mind that books were not worth while, and, restless and dissatisfied, I threw them aside and determined to see life from a totally different angle. With the longing for the hills, of which I have spoken, strong within me, I cast about for some occupation that would take me back to them and I hit upon shawl trading. This had the added advantage of the appeal, or the excuse, of usefulness to my family, who made no objection to my going. Fortunately for me, Indian life gives ample opportunity to an unquiet spirit, and, as I have said, there is nothing in our thought or our tradition to bind a restless young man in search of truth to one place or occupation. The significance of the vows I had taken was spiritual and the profession of the priesthood incidental. Had not my holy man enjoined me to find God through play? And something of a play it was to go with the caravans into the Himalayas and bring back shawls. I wore a turban made by one of the Cashmereans, which cost an enormous amount of money. My shawl was one of the richest ever made, and I had a servant with me. I must have had in those days something of the Western idea of advertising.

One day in the Himalayas this amazing thing happened: I had left a shawl on a rock and forgotten all about it. Six days later I remembered it and came back, and there was the shawl exactly where I had put it!

I said to an old man in the neighborhood, "Father, why didn't anybody steal that shawl?"

"Thieving grows in the poisonous air of the valley; never in our hills," he replied.

Once in a hill town I met a beautiful dancer. Everyone wanted her to dance for him. To whom would she grant the favor? All the young men were bringing her presents so I, thinking to outdo them, took one of my most beautiful and costly shawls and bore it proudly to her house. Two musicians were in attendance, and there was a hookah, but in those days I did not know how to smoke. The dancer came to me and looked at the shawl I had brought her, then she put her finger under my chin and said, "Little brother, go home! You haven't yet finished drinking the milk of innocence." And I went home with my shawl, humiliated.

Returning from the hills after selling all my wares, I traveled by railroad. Now traveling by railroad in India, as everyone knows who has read *Kim*, is a picturesque experience, and I threw myself with youthful zest into every encounter. Here was play indeed, for a common experience like a railroad journey produces in people of different race and language the most surprising and amusing contacts that can be imagined.

One day I was waiting on the platform for a train to come. After three hours the train was heard. It stopped at a distance and whistled for the signal to come into the station.

The man who gives the signals was eating his dinner and he grumbled, "What does it want, the fool, screeching like that?"

"It wants a signal to come to the platform," somebody said.

"Then let it wait till I've finished my dinner," replied the man crossly.

When you get into a car and the train is about to start, a guard walks up and down, calling to the people to keep their heads and arms inside. "Do not stick your arms out; they might be broken!" So the people stick out their legs just to be contrary, and laugh at his warnings.

When the train stops at a station everybody crowds to windows and platform to fill their bowls with water which a vendor distributes. And at the same time you will hear the cry, "Beef and bread! Beef and bread!" And the Mohammedans go to the window and say, "Bring us meat. Bring us lots of it. There are too many Hindus in this car. We want more room." These Mohammedans, who are fat, spread themselves out in the train to eat their meat, and all the Hindus shrink back into the corners to be as far away as possible and avoid pollution, and so the Mohammedans get all the room they want.

Once I was traveling on a very crowded train. A lot of men were going to Calcutta to work during the autumn; they had left their wives behind, and they were feeling lonely and homesick and rather grouchy. Then a young man got into the train, bringing his wife with him. This excited them all very much and they began asking shrilly, "What is he doing with his bride? We have to leave our wives at home and behold this man indulges in the extravagance of bringing his with him! Let them stand; it serves them right!" But a man from a minor province—a Kayath said solemnly, "There must be respect shown to a woman." He got up and gave her his seat. He used, however, the Kayath word for woman, *meraru,* and one of the Hindus, eager to pick a quarrel and relieve his feelings, said, "Thou dost not even know the proper word! Who stoops to understand Kayathi!" But the young wife, evidently a bride of about sixteen, could contain herself no longer and took her seat with great dignity announcing sententiously to the Kayath, but loud enough for the whole car to hear, "No matter what the language, everyone understands when the son of a hero-mother speaks!" It had the desired effect; after that everyone was overcome, and perfect silence reigned in the car.

The couple needed milk, but the husband was very shy and when the train stopped he would not go and get it; he said they could do without. So she went to the window and bargained with the milk woman.

Proud of her recent victory, and wishing to display her knowledge of the world, she began belligerently, "What kind of water dost thou put in the milk, ditch water or river water, I would like to know?"

But the old milk woman was equal to her: "O thou childless one, my own children drink this milk. Dost thou suppose in thy ignorance that children drink watered milk?"

The bride asked rather nervously, "How knowest thou that I am childless?"

"Thy impudence betokens barrenness."

The bride lost her temper. "If I had thy age I would have twice as many children as thou—take thy money and give me the milk." Her dignity regained with the last word, she drank, then gave the milk to her husband. But he did not like to have people see that he was drinking from the same cup that his wife had used, for he was very shy; and so he said, "I am not thirsty," But his wife made him drink it. Said she, "Oh, drink thy milk and be quiet!" And so it went, back and forth between the occupants of that car all the way to Calcutta.

At another time, we had come across the Ganges on a boat, and we were taking the train. But we noticed that on all the cars had been marked: "Reserved." There was not a single compartment left. I made up my mind I must get to my destination somehow, so I went into the train and found a car with bunks, and being agile, I slipped up on top of one. Gradually the car filled below.

Some soldiers came in and put their luggage under the benches and sat down and began to talk. "It's wonderful that our prince has whole compartments reserved for us," said one importantly.

"Our prince is a fool," retorted another.

DHAN GOPAL MUKERJI

"He couldn't have had the brains to think this out: some fool in his administration gave them to us."

"If there are so many fools doing good to us, nobody need be wise," said the first.

"Dost thou not know it is the railway's courtesy shown to the prince's regiment which gives us the car?" said a third soldier, with a convincing air of knowledge, and so they chattered until noticing me on top, one of them called up, "But who is this brother-in-law sleeping up there?"

Now "brother-in-law" is a very abusive word in India. They were big men; I knew any one of them could kill two of me and they were the rajah's soldiers. Hoping to carry off the situation, I scrambled up and looking over asked pertly, "Who wishes to be related to me?"

"Ah," said one, fortunately amused by my impudence, "a little gentleman has come in. When didst thou finish drinking milk?"

"Long before thou didst learn to wear clothes," I retorted. So down I came and we talked about their country. Later they went to sleep and I climbed back again and went to sleep too in my former place.

We reached our destination. The first thing we heard was "Water! Water!" Everybody took water. Then came the call: "Beef and bread." The Mohammedans, of whom there were only a few in the train, had their dinner and as soon as they had finished eating their meat, the Hindus, who had filled their pitchers with water, poured it on the heads of the Mohammedans, saying, "Now be cleansed, O you sons of pigs!" The Mohammedans were furious, but the train started on again, and the soldiers said, "It is a wise thought to cleanse the Mohammedans when Hindus are in the majority!" And so moved the ever-changing pageant in which I was both actor and audience.

The people who have the most difficulty in railroad travel are the poor Mohammedan ladies, obliged to go so closely veiled that they can hardly see to get on and off the trains. One day I saw a Mohammedan gentleman pushing a way for himself and his three wives through the crowded platform toward the Bombay mail. He reached the train, which was booked to leave in ninety seconds, and began trying to hurry his first wife into a compartment. She was a rotund, somewhat elderly, and very voluminous person, and it was quick work to push her up the steps in sixty seconds. Then came number two, slighter in build but equally enveloped, but by a miracle the Mohammedan gentleman shoved her into a place in thirty seconds; then the engine whistled. The third wife frightened and breathless was just putting her foot on the step behind her husband when the guard pushed by, shoving them both to the platform and slamming the door. He waved his green flag to the engine driver and the unfortunate Mohammedan, seeing two of his wives about to be carried away cried out, "For the love of Allah, restore my two wives or let us get in!"

"Isn't one wife enough for you?" replied the guard unsympathetically, and the train started to pull out.

The two agitated ladies in the car had dragged off their veils in their effort to see what was happening to them, and their husband turned from the guard to scream at them, "Hide your faces, hide your faces, shameless ones! Would you disgrace me in a railway station?"

All the doors were closed, all the passengers in, the guard was climbing into his car, the last on the train, but the now frantic Mohammedan rushed after him and shouting, "Thou shalt not go with my two wives!" held him in a firm embrace as the train moved slowly out of the station. Then at last the frustrated guard waved the red flag to make the train come back. The last I saw through the car window was the heads of the united family bobbing wildly as for the second time the train moved out.

Full of such incidents my journeyings were, and rich in character and in color, vastly amusing to the boy that I still was, but at the end of the months of travel, in spite of the mighty background of the hills, in spite of the throb of humanity beneath their serene summits, I was still a wanderer, and no nearer a goal than when I had started. I had had some dim hope behind my youthful zest for adventure, that I might meet the supreme experience in the hills, and find, among the many hermits who flock to the Himalayas in search of God, a master greater than I had known before, who would tell me, with all the detail so dear to the heart of youth, the meaning of my life, and point out to me my way. But, alas, I did not find the mighty spirit wandering alone and saying to himself, "Therefore, O my soul, wander alone like a rhinoceros!" And very soon I wearied of the shawls and returned home, disappointed like many another youth before me, to enter the University of Calcutta.

XI

My Brother's Marriage

S hortly after my return, one of my brothers was married.
Marriages in India are arranged by the parents. The young people are told at a certain time that they are to be married; only then are they introduced to each other and asked whether they like each other or not. They generally say yes, and soon after, the marriage is celebrated.

Now in olden times, before the conquest of India by the Mohammedans, women chose their own husbands. It used to be called *sayamvara* meaning "the choice." If the king's daughter was to be married, all the kings and princes would come to the king's door, and the maiden would choose her husband from amongst them. A story is told to Hindu children even now which illustrates the ancient custom:

In times long ago there was a king in India who had a fair daughter named Sanyukta. Now Sanyukta's nurse, who had brought her up, always told her wonderful tales about a certain king in Northern India named Prithvi—of his beauty, and of his valor, exceeding that of all other men, and as the girl grew into glorious maidenhood, she had only Prithvi's image in her heart. But the king, her father, was at war with Prithvi and she never saw her heart's idol.

One day the news went forth that the time had come for the Princess Sanyukta to choose a husband, and all the princes of India who had visited her father's court, assembled together to contest for her hand. The nurse, knowing whose image was graven in Sanyukta's heart, went forth to the kingdom of Prithvi and reaching the king, persuaded him to disguise himself as a beggar and go to the assembly where Princess Sanyukta was to choose a husband.

When all the princes of India were arranged in accordance to their rank, the portals opened, and Sanyukta walked out of the palace. Her father and mother watched from the upper balconies, eager to know whom she would choose. She passed the most wealthy princes, and then the most valorous and the most powerful; though the attendants of each prince sang his praise, Sanyukta passed on unheeding. She came at last to the princes whose pretentions were greater than either their wisdom or their prowess, and still she did not choose. Her parents were terribly anxious. "Is our daughter going to reject them all?" said they.

Now, the old king, to mock his enemy Prithvi before all these princes, had put a wooden image of him at the end of the court, and when the Princess reached that image, she stopped in front of it and put a garland at its feet.

"What an insult to offer to the Princes of India," cried the nobles.

Then a beggar concealed all this time in their midst rose and cried, "It is not an insult, but a challenge! I am Prithvi. She has chosen me!" His white charger was near. He took the girl in his arms and leaped on his war-horse and galloped away to his home.

That is what my old nurse told me regarding the ancient system. This is the last tale of marriage by choice in India. Prithvi was conquered and killed by the Mohammedans. From that day on men and women had no time to choose one another. It was necessary to find a system of marriage by which the men could protect the women from the invading Mohammedans, for the Mohammedans intended to convert all India to Mohammedanism, and since the Hindus were not willing converts but resisted to the point of death, the only way open was to force Hindu women to bear Mohammedan children. As the law of the sword had failed to convert India, the Mohammedans thought they could succeed by the law of nature. Being polygamous the advantage was on their side. But when the Hindu men died fighting, the entire female population of garrison towns, in order not to fall into the hands of their conquerors, burned themselves alive. It was this measure that saved India from being overpopulated by Mohammedan children. To this day the Hindus are in the majority. The eight hundred years of Mohammedan rule saw in India a new marriage system totally unlike the ancient *sayamvara*. Girls before they reached the age of maturity were irrevocably betrothed to young Hindus, so that they could be protected from the Mohammedan enemy. And it is this system of marriage that has prevailed until the end of the nineteenth century.

Today young people are told to marry each other and they do so. If there is any love it is after marriage, not before. In this respect young people in America and Europe have a great advantage. They at least have love before marriage, no matter what happens later.

In India, after the young people have seen each other, the betrothal ceremony is held. But this is no simple matter. The astrologers have to search their horoscopes to see whether the stars under which they were born are harmonious. If the stars are not harmonious, the marriage does not take place. Sometimes it almost seems as if it were the stars and not the young people who were to be mated!

No marriage takes place in the day time; they always wait for evening when the stars are out. The astrologers enjoy the marriages quite as much as, if not more than, anybody else. They like to forecast all kinds of terrible things and sometimes they come true, the four times they are right keeping out of the minds of people the ninety-six times they are wrong!

Every family has attached to it from generation to generation a family of matchmakers. And this is a very curious institution. These men are able to enumerate all the diseases of each member of their employer's family and the information is handed down from father to son. They are a singular people, hiding considerable astuteness and worldly wisdom behind a kind of buffoonery, always attaching to their profession, which makes them fill at times a rôle not unlike the old European jester's.

When the time came for my brother to marry, our matchmaker was called in to find a wife for him, as my parents did not know where to look for a suitable one. The matchmaker, typical of his kind, stood and gazed at the ceiling, then gazed down, and tapped his head three times with his forefinger. After a very profound pause, he remarked, "The diseases of this family are not of a very violent order. Let me see: has there been any insanity in the last seven generations?"

"There has been none," my grandfather answered.

Then the matchmaker asked, "Who was the young girl who used to have fits of biting people?"

My grandfather replied to this characteristic witticism, "Art thou truly the grandson of him who made the match for me, or art thou descended from a he-ass?"

And the matchmaker answered, "Now I know I must go to a fool's nest to find a bride fit for such a family as this!" and tapping his head three times again, off he went. In a short time he brought news of a maiden whose father was rich, and in whose family, after consulting the matchmaker and obtaining his inherited information, our matchmaker said there were no dangerous diseases.

Then my parents made the next move and called upon the parents of the girl, asking them if they had any objection to a marriage between my brother and their daughter. After that my father took my brother with him and paid a formal visit to the young girl. She was thirteen years old. When my brother returned from the call, he remarked, "She does not shine like gold, nor is she made of brass."

And so it was settled, and one night we all went to the maiden's house prepared for the long ceremonial, and armed with a retinue of relatives, priests and followers, including our matchmaker and astrologer as well as our poet and our philosopher, for every family would think itself disgraced on such an occasion without the services of poetry and philosophy. Of course, long before this the astrologers had settled the hour for the marriage, and the compatibility of the stars under which the young couple were born.

We accompanied the bridegroom to the place where the altar fires were burning. He stood there while the bride was brought in, seated in a sandal-wood chair and carried by her four brothers. The seat of the chair was covered with beautiful lotus designs drawn by the most skillful woman of the bride's family. These designs signified: "May you step from lotus to lotus all your life." The bride's eyes were veiled. First she was carried round the fire seven times, and then it was my brother's turn to go around the fire.

Now they stood facing each other at the altar and then came the solemn and beautiful moment of the ceremony. He swore: "By my parents, by the deities of the family, by the One God, I will cherish and protect and love thee, and even if thou wert faithless to me, I would wait until the eternal self overcame the temporal self. What more shall I say? Not only in this incarnation but through all the incarnations to come, mayst thou be tied to me, as the beating is tied to the heart!" She repeated this vow after him. Again they encircled the fire seven times, and then they were asked for their final consent. A veil was put over their heads and they looked at each other under it for a minute or more. This is called "the good look" or "the consenting look." Even then one of them could have withdrawn, but beyond that there is no divorce, not even on the grounds of infidelity. The priest asked them again, "Do you swear that after this look you are satisfied?" And they affirmed their vows. The elders rose. The boy and girl joined their hands and said together: "Thy flesh on my flesh; thy hands on my hands; thy heart on my heart; and our two hearts fastened on the heart of God. Thus shall it be."

Then as a symbol of unity he put on her hand two conch shell bracelets. The bracelets are made of this material so that the rich and poor can have the same emblem of marriage. When a woman becomes a widow, she breaks her conch bracelets.

The ceremony was over. We all sat and dined together. We fed the poor of the community and the unfortunate, which is a custom always observed on the day of a wedding.

After the feasting, the next event in the celebration was matching the family philosophers—ours against theirs, and our poet against their poet. The silent discussion between the philosophers was typical of these occasions. Their philosopher raised two fingers and our philosopher raised one, meaning: "You say God is two?" "I say God is one!" Their philosopher raised five fingers and our philosopher raised a little finger; they meant: "Are the five elements God?" "No, He is the smallest of the small because He is the greatest of the great." Then their philosopher showed his fist with the thumb in, meaning: "God is in the world," and our philosopher showed his open palm, meaning: "He is in all things, yet nothing can contain Him." We wearied after a while of the silent debate, and set our two poets on each other like hungry dogs. Their egotism was suffering while the philosophers held the stage.

Our poet said, "Give me the first word"; and their poet answered, "Ganges." Our poet replied instantly, "She is the sea-lover, yet when she finds the sea she is homesick for her cradle of the snows, and seeking to return to them she makes the rising tides. Now I will give the word and you must compose a verse. My word is 'the swan.'" Their poet did not compose, but he quoted something magnificent: "The swan of immortality goes out through the senses into the waters of silence. He is the secret of secrets. He is the dumbness in the speech of man and the speech in the dumbness of animals."

Next came a play, "The Song of Songs." This is the usual ritual followed at weddings. Apparently the play is given to illustrate the meaning of life. The Song of Songs describes how Krishna falls in love with Radha, who kindles his senses though she is unable to satisfy him. He wants other women and so is led astray, but he finds that the senses cannot give him what the soul requires. Radha is waiting, and Krishna, after wandering through the wilderness of sensuality, finally returns to her, and cries, "If you will say the word that forgives, it will unfetter me from my illusions. Around me coils the dragon of my darkness; cleave it with the scimitar of your speech! Your beauty is steeper than the sky and my soul goes forth like a moon-bird to meet you. But why are you so far away? You are the pang of my heart, and the thought that scars me; come down, O humbler of heights! I am Radha-mad; un-Radha me not, O my Radha!"

In that Song of Songs with its beautiful verse, the whole meaning of the Indian marriage is expressed, which reduced from poetry to prose, indicates that the soul passes through its sensuous experience so that the senses may be lifted to the level of the soul. At a certain period in the lives of two people their senses unite them and through the ensuing exaltation their souls are led into a common understanding of all experience. That is love, and love has nothing to do with the time process of this world. Though it may go astray, ultimately it returns. Nothing can steal it, nothing can subtract from it. The senses help the soul to grow from the beautiful to the good, from the good to the true, from the true to the holy. The purpose of love and marriage is to help souls to grow from the least comprehensive to the most comprehensive experience.

In a Sanskrit play "Sakuntala" the Indian idea of marriage is expressed in another way. Sakuntala means "the forgotten self" or "the forgotten face." In this play the king goes to the jungle to kill deer. He strays into a hermitage which is kept by the adopted daughter of the hermit, whose name is Sakuntala. The king falls in love with her and they are married. After a time the king returns to his city and she waits in vain for a message from him. One day Sakuntala is in the garden meditating upon her lord, and when a saint asks for hospitality, she does not hear him. He, therefore, curses her, saying, "The one you are thinking of will forget you." (Saints in no other countries lose their temper so often as in India—and Ireland.) She rouses herself and begs his forgiveness and is told that the curse will endure for a time, but that when the king recognizes something which he had given her, he will remember his bride again.

Months later while the girl is on a journey in search of the king, her ring, given her by him, drops into the river and a fish swallows it. Later a fisherman is arrested for stealing the king's ring. He is brought to court and pleads that he found it in the mouth of a fish which he had caught. The king looks at the ring, recognizing it as the one which he had given to Sakuntala. Remembering then his beloved, he sets forth to look for her, but in vain. At last he comes to the jungle and finds a boy playing with lion cubs. Thinking to himself, "This boy is royal, for he is playing with the cubs of the jungle king," he asks the boy for his father. "I have no father, but I know my mother," replies the lad. Then he brings the king to his mother's house and the king recognizes his wife and they are united once more.

Thus the forgotten face is remembered, and the soul finds again what it had never really lost.

Here we notice the characteristic self-abnegation of the Indian. If anything goes wrong with the world, it is the individual not the world who is to blame.

But to return to the bride and groom who after the play had gone into the house. There the ladies were chaffing the bridegroom while the bride looked on. It is the custom in India for the bride's elder sister to tease the bridegroom with all sorts of embarrassing questions, something in this wise: "Can you sing a song?" asked my sister-in-law.

My brother answered quickly, "How can I? Your beauty has sealed my lips."

Then another sister-in-law coaxed, "Tell us a story!"

But my brother shook his head saying, "I am dumb, for the story of my heart is just beginning!"

Back and forth they chaffed each other further. "What college degrees have you?"

"The degree of imbecility!"

"Do you know how to love?"

"If you have taught your sister how!"

"In our family love is real; we need no teaching."

"No wonder, for it is my family that has always taught yours!"

The night was passed in such pleasantries. In the morning the bride and groom came to our house, but she returned the same day. From that time on until she was fifteen, my brother went to see her every afternoon, and thus they grew into a beautiful friendship before the marriage was consummated.

When my sister-in-law at last came to keep house, my mother received her and gave her a key as a symbol of the family, saying, "The key: the symbol of wifehood, motherhood, womanhood, I give it to you. I hope I have passed it on to you as I have received it."

In coming to our house, the bride did not step on the ground. Rugs and shawls and such things were spread from her old home to her new, so that she touched no dust but that of her new house. The whole house was strewn with flowers this evening, called the "flower evening" when the bride enters her husband's house, and she and my brother wore the nuptial robes that had been in our family for generations. Then the bride, to signify that she would never let the flower of chastity die out, put a brand into the family oven, which in our house, as in most Indian houses, is fed by a fire kept alive from generation to generation. Then in order to leave the place free to the young people, my parents went on a pilgrimage for a while.

We believe in India that woman is man's spiritual superior, though physically man is her protector. In matters of religion woman is supreme; in matters of politics man is the master. A man never interferes with a woman's sphere. In the household her will is law. For instance, a man would refuse to wear no charms, however strange in shape, on his neck and arms if a woman of his house fastened them there. When he leaves the house in the morning it is the custom for a man to ask "Godspeed" from his wife. But if he does not take her blessing, it is the woman who fasts, to expiate his neglect.

This is the Indian ideal of love and marriage, but irregularities sometimes occur. A man we knew very well was in love with a dancer, and for a long time could not escape that infatuation. His wife said to him, "I want you to promise me one thing only. Always bathe in the Ganges before you come home to me." Two or three years later this man found himself. Someone asked his wife how it happened. "You see," she said, "I knew that his infidelity was but a veil drawn over his spirit. The only way I could remind him of this was to have him bathe in the Ganges, so that the cleansing of the body might bring about a cleansing of the soul." The word for wife in India is *sahadharmini*, meaning "leader in spirituality" or "companion of the soul."

XII

East and West

There is a gulf between the oriental and the occidental mind: it is as though each were a lighthouse on a separate headland, illuminating the channel on one side and the channel on the other, but leaving in complete darkness the crossing between. This crossing I was about to attempt, though at the time of which I write—a period shortly after my brother's marriage—I had no idea of the adventure before me, or that I stood at the beginning of so great a change.

Our large family was scattered. I was hard at my studies in the University of Calcutta and struggling against the boredom with which my teachers inspired me. Study could not help me, my soul still hungered for space, for some unattainable good that remained unrealized except as a continual goad to my eager, unsatisfied spirit. My mother's health was failing, and home was sad to me. Then as a climax to all this, my gifted poet brother, a young man of great promise, died. Though I did not guess it at the time, this was to end my life at home. My mother was greatly affected by the loss of this beloved son; he was very close to her in sympathy. He was full of the power of his inspiration and often when a child and tired of my lessons, I used to seek him out and watch him write. He would be very slow about it. First an unintelligible word would fly in from nowhere and alight on the white sheet of paper. Then would come another word and sit next it. It would always upset the meanings I had associated with the first word, which would be further confused by more words alighting one by one in front of it. Then suddenly the last word would fly in and take its final place and that would lift the veil like a juggler, and the flaming sentence golden with meaning and beauty would dance before my eyes.

All ties seemed to me loosened after his death. My mother's health failed more and more rapidly—life was very dark. I cast about for some way in which to lose myself and the consciousness of my distress. One of my remaining brothers had thrown himself heart and soul into the nationalist movement and India's industrial future, and when I found a worthy cause in this brother's hopes for India, I embraced it eagerly and the new-born nationalism took entire possession of me. My mother too was in sympathy; her heart responded to the idea of working for India though she was unable to grapple with our desire to improve India by means of Western materialism. To her mind so simple, yet as I now realize, so much more mature than ours, it was more important to insure our country's religious heritage than to acquire the riches of this world. But she was willing to accept what my brother and I, in our high hope, believed to be possible—the attainment of the kingdom of heaven once we could compete with the European in his own field.

So when I was offered a chance to go to Japan to study industrial machinery in order to learn Western scientific methods of production, I did not hesitate. We were given a traveling scholarship. My mother bade me go and said, characteristically, "Go, my son, and study the inner experience of time and make it your own. If that gives you the verity underlying the time process, embrace it. He who has set my feet upon the path of the timeless, is waiting to meet you where the path of time ends."

I was soon to find that my mother had as usual struck to the heart of the matter, and how hard it was to reconcile an alien evolution with the oriental's innate conception of the meaning of time. The West believes in time, in the time process, and consequently, in cause and effect, then in results, then in good and evil. But the East begins by denying the fundamental reality of time, which necessarily changes for us the relative importance of all that results from time. This is the essential difference between the East and the West.

I had a talk once with my holy man which perhaps will serve to make this more clear. We were sitting under a tree together when we saw a Western gentleman hastening by. I asked my master, "Why do the Western people run?"

He answered, "Don't you see? They think the road has an end, and that they must be there before the rest of the world, while we know that the road has no end, so we sit still and meditate." Then he quoted: "He is more still than the mountains, yet swifter than the swiftest flight of man's mind; the sun rises and sets, but it is only a golden mask on the face of the truth."

Later on I ran for a train and missed it. I said to the gatekeeper, "If I had run faster I could have caught it!"

He replied, "How long have you waited around in this station?"

"Since last night," said I.

He remarked jovially, "If you had come night before last, you would undoubtedly have caught it."

So I went home and asked my holy man, "You say the time process is unreal; then why did I miss my train?"

He answered, "I never said the time process is unreal."

"O Holy One, then it *is* real?" said I.

"It is real to those who have experienced its reality."

"Have you experienced this reality?"

He said, "No; in an assembly of fools, I have sat still."

Then I asked him, "But suppose *you* were to catch a train?"

He said, "I would trap it as a fowler traps a bird; I would master it, but I would never let it trap me! The time process is real in the sense that bathing on a hot day is real, but when it is done, the rest of the day is for meditation."

Here are some further illustrations of the differences that exist between East and West:

Once at Benares I stopped to bathe in the Ganges and I saw an old priest who had taken his bath and was meditating. The sun was out and he was basking in it and evidently enjoying himself, when up to him came rushing two Americans, a man and a girl. The man put his hand on this beautiful, benevolent priest and said, "Wait a minute, Jim," and pointed his camera at him. He added reassuringly. "Don't be scared; it won't bite!" Then snapping his picture, he hastily put a coin in the old man's hand and disappeared as suddenly as he had come. The priest, who had been meditating upon the Lord, looked at the coin, then looked at the disappearing people. In silence he threw the coin into the water. He had been polluted by its touch. After that he went into the Ganges and took another bath and meditated another half hour.

There is a district in my part of India where people used to make Dacca gauze, or Indian muslin, which is very valuable. But then cheap machinery gauze of the West came in and destroyed their industry. The people could not compete with the machine-made gauze, and so, in order to gain a living, they went into the making of gunny sacks, from jute. In course of time the jute industry failed and then they tried to make muslin again, but their sense of touch had been destroyed by the roughness of the jute. About five thousand people had lost this touch, which had taken thousands of years to create. Their livelihood was gone, and a beautiful art lost to the race.

My grandfather used to tell me, that when a man wanted to borrow money from another man in the old days before the English came, his servant would go to the other man's servant and talk it over. Then the lender would slip the money under his friend's doorstep at night so that the borrower would not be humiliated. If the borrower did not pay, the creditor would go and do *danna,* which means fasting at the door of the debtor. After a few days' fasting even the most conscienceless debtor was brought to pay his debts. Today we have stamps and signed notes, and all such proceedings, yet even so, we do not pay our debts. In one hundred years of Western rule, the moral outlook has gone, because stamps are there in place of morality. Macaulay, the stupidest man of genius the Lord ever made, gave the British law to India to take the place of our old complicated, unworkable system of law procedure. British law has been a tremendous convenience in clearing up affairs—it produces order. The British think they have brought justice to India, but the Hindus, being orientals (as Jesus Christ was) think that no human being can do justice. "Judge not that ye be not judged." A man has only one thing to offer to his fellow man for any offense he may commit, and that is compassion.

I was convinced, however, of my ability to understand both the Eastern and Western approaches to life and I bravely set forth upon my way, bravely, that is, except for my farewells. I told no one but my mother of the date of my departure. The day before, she said to me, "I think you will do very little when you go to Japan. The song is in the throat of the bird; the bird will not find it by wandering in the sky."

Then I asked her, "What shall I do to make you happy?"

She waited a moment and said quietly, "Keep the doors of your mind open, so that not one of God's truths will have to go away because the door is shut." And then she gave me her blessing.

The day I started I had not the courage to say goodbye to her. I knew that if I saw her once more I should never leave. Yet though broken and dying her orders were that I should go. I felt sure I should never see my mother again and I was right. She lingered another year and died. I knew when it happened although I did not hear the news until weeks afterward. I was plunged in sorrow. Then suddenly, one day thinking of her, the certainty of God and immortality rushed upon me—no longer an idea but an experience, and since then my consciousness of her is freed from any entanglement of life and death.

After arriving in Japan, I began my studies in textile engineering. It seemed the nearest way of getting the experience I desired. We were ordered to enter the factory at seven, and to leave at six, except twice a month, when we had a holiday of twenty-four hours.

When the cherry blossoms came in April, we were given three days' holiday to go and look at them. The worship of the beautiful in Japan is extraordinary. It seems they believe only in beauty, not in morality, not in spirituality, and yet when one stands before the Buddha in Kamura, which is a perfect work of art, it gives a deep experience of holiness.

After these three days' vacation I received my first shock from the time process. As one of the girls was tending a machine which I happened to be drawing, she made a careless gesture and her hand was caught in the wheel. Suddenly I saw her face turn white and heard a terrible shriek of pain. My first instinct was to run to her, but instead I had to run to the engineer to bid him stop the machinery. When I returned to the girl, she was sitting on the floor holding a mangled arm with her other hand. Soon the other operators came and took her away. The strangest thing is how little the Japanese cry. I remember that this girl sat on the floor and swayed with closed eyes nursing her mangled hand. I heard afterwards that she was paid five hundred yen or two hundred and fifty dollars for this mishap. But what troubled me most was that when her place was taken by another girl, we never mentioned in our conversation the one who had gone. It seemed as if we were as callous towards our fellow beings as the machines were to us.

I soon gave up this work and decided to choose a happier vehicle through which to experience the time process. At this juncture I met an Indian who had been in America. He said, "Japan is no country for anybody; if you want to see the civilized use of machinery, go to America." Then he drew an Arabian Nights' picture of the United States. He said, "Anyone who doesn't like America had better freeze up and get out! No son-of-a-gun that is a knocker need apply there!" His language sounded extremely romantic after the Miltonic English to which I had been accustomed, and I felt irresistibly drawn to America. But I stayed about Japan four months longer, because I had not the decision to move, and I spent all my money except just enough to cover my passage to San Francisco. Finally I set forth again to meet this most tremendous change of all, having broken the ties of my country, my past and my caste. For alien though I found Japan to be, it was still an oriental country, but now I was to reach a place where I could keep none of my traditions. Some of this I understood, but I had no conception of the changes that were to come.

PART II

OUTCAST

I

INITIATION INTO AMERICA

America at last! The seventeen days of Asiatic steerage seemed like the experience of another man the very moment the immigration authorities gave me permission to enter the United States. The reverence that I felt for this country was so great that nothing short of falling on my knees and kissing its soil would have sufficed to express my feelings. But Americans are a strange people! No sooner did they see that I had such feelings for their country than they began to knock it out of me in a very unceremonious fashion.

The first American I met on landing was a man very quaintly dressed (later on I learned he was wearing "overalls"), who had been sent to me to take care of my trunk. I gave him my trunk, which he threw from the deck of the ship down to the wharf—a matter of some eight or ten feet. Not knowing enough colloquial English, I quoted to him the magnificent lines of Milton: "Him the Almighty Power hurled headlong flaming from the ethereal sky." The expressman looked at me very quizzically and exclaimed: "Cut it out! You're too fresh!" This was my initiation into America.

Somebody directed me to a boarding house where I spent the night. When I was called to breakfast the next morning I noticed the sugar was missing from the table. When after some fuss the landlady produced the sugar, I said to her: "This reduces the entire discussion to a *reductio ad absurdum*," she exclaimed: "My God, what's that?"

Since I had come to acquire knowledge in America, I did not tarry in the seaport town very long, but hastened to Berkeley, the site of the University of California. I had no money except fifteen dollars that a friend had lent me. I went to the university hungry for knowledge, not knowing that knowledge, like bread, has to be paid for. So they took fourteen dollars out of my fifteen under different pretences, such as "nonresident fee," "gymnasium fee," and "infirmary fee," and to my great consternation, that drew my last dollar out of my pocket, as the magnet draws the needle, for I had spent the fifteenth dollar already; and there was nothing left! Yet thanks to a fellow traveler on the ship, I did have the care of friends. I had met on the ship a young Jewish-American named

Barusch who one afternoon came down from his second-class deck to talk with me in the steerage. A quotation I had occasion to use from Emerson astonished him and he exclaimed "Why, you are an educated man." Being young, I answered, "Yes—very." That made him take pity on me and he invited me to come upstairs and have tea with him. Tea parties with him became after that daily affairs of more importance than I was ready to acknowledge. They were the only occasions when I ate anything, during the entire trip, because in the Asiatic steerage they gave us Japanese food which I simply could not swallow.

When I decided to go to Berkeley, young Barusch, who was planning to stay on in Seattle, gave me a note to his family who lived in Oakland. They were kind enough to put me up for seven days. I never told them how little money I had, and since I could not buy any presents I gave them, as an expression of my gratitude, the few Indian rugs and Japanese vases I had brought in my trunk. I am positive had they known how little I possessed they would have refused everything, for they were the kindest and most generous of people.

But I could not go on exchanging Indian art for American food and so I sought out a Hindu student, who told me to go and get a job. Apparently he had lived in America a very long time. I asked him what kind of a job. He said, "Dishwashing, taking care of the house—anything. Go and ring the bell of every house until you find a job." So I went on ringing door bell after door bell. From each opening door came a "No thank you," in tones running the whole scale from the snarl of a tiger to the smile of a lady.

But at last I reached a house where they asked, "What can you do?"

"Anything," I said—"washing dishes, taking care of the house."

"Can you begin tomorrow?" the lady asked me.

I replied that I could, but I must first find lodging for the night. "May I come to you?" I politely inquired.

In a very businesslike way she replied, "All right. Your room will be ready in the back yard."

So I hastened back the same afternoon with my bundle and one book, a copy of Emerson's *Self-Reliance*. I was shown into a little cabin in the backyard and was given a badly needed meal, for I had had nothing to eat all day.

Next day my duties began. I did manage to clean the house somehow. I swept the front porch and swept the back porch, but it never entered my head to take the dust away on the dust pan, and I swept all the dust from the house onto the sidewalk. My employer's neighbor telephoned her that the sidewalk must be kept clean, as it is a state law. I hastened then, in my shirt sleeves, with my suspenders showing, to sweep off the sidewalk. But my employer stopped me and said: "Don't shame the house by going out like that. Put on your jacket." I had never heard a coat called a jacket before, so she had to explain to me, and by the time I had understood, most of the dust had been removed by the wind.

However, this employment did not last long. By noon time a huge pile of dishes had accumulated in the kitchen to be washed and my employer said to me during lunch, "Perhaps you want to wait until your lunch is over before washing the dishes." I hastily assented and began eating lunch. After lunch I piled up more dishes in the sink, put on my coat, and went out for a walk in the beautiful sunshine. When I had returned from my walk, my employer sternly demanded, "Why aren't the dishes done?"

I said, "How do you wash them?"

"Don't you know?" she asked in astonishment.

I said, "No."

"But," she said, "you took the job on the understanding that you would wash dishes."

"I will wash dishes if you will show me how," I replied.

Then in great dudgeon she said, "Will you please look for another place tomorrow?"

"What place?" I asked.

She answered, "I mean you are fired."

I asked again, "What is 'fired?'" And I was told, "In good English, you are discharged!" "But," she added with a smile, "you can stay here tonight."

And so I sat in the kitchen chair and watched her wash the dishes. I watched her very carefully to see what steps led up to the washing and wiping of dishes, deciding to make use of my lesson in my next place.

I was so chagrined at having lost my place that I made up my mind not to accept the invitation to spend another night in the house of my defeat but to set out without more delay in search of another job. So the same ringing of bells and the same snarls and barks from different doors began again for me. At one house, after the servant opened the door in answer to the bell and I told her what I wanted, she slammed the door with a great noise. I paused and said to myself, "This is what they mean in the English idiom when they say in novels: 'She shut the door in his face.'" I distinctly remember that the door almost touched the tip of my nose when it was banged to.

However, in a little while I succeeded in finding a place where I could begin work the next morning. This time it was washing dishes, waiting on table, and washing knives and forks. In exchange for this I was given my room and board free. And I must remind the reader now, that I was going to college as well, for the university had just opened and instruction had begun.

In my new place I washed the morning dishes very well. There was no waiting on table at breakfast. It was a boy's club and they seemed rather nice and noisy. I never knew people could make so much noise getting ready for classes. The racket was terrible. At luncheon came my first experience at waiting on table and I was very nervous. They gave me a plate of soup to put before a boy. I hastened from the kitchen into the dining room and as I was putting the plate down it struck the boy's head and the soup went down his back. And then I received my first lesson in what might be called the American language! The Chinese cook, at once understanding that I knew nothing of waiting on table, put on the white jacket which he had given to me, and waited on table himself. I watched him from the door and was filled with amazement to see a man putting a plate of soup down before another man without the slightest trembling of the hand. The cook felt kindly towards me and so he taught me many things concerning waiting on table, the washing of dishes and the polishing of knives and forks.

But I lost this job because of something very different from inexperience. I found that every day the cook invented new work for me to do. From waiting on table and washing silver I was asked to wash the glasses and since I learned to do that well, I was asked to wipe the kitchen dishes after the cook had washed them. I feared lest pretty soon I might be asked to cook as well. So one day in great exasperation I threw up the job. This was the first inkling I got that employers could be immoral.

Again I began to look for a job and after a few fruitless hours of search I found an excellent position in a fraternity: room and board and ten dollars a month for washing dishes, waiting on table and making beds. But I did not have to make the beds the first two days because the boy they had employed previously stayed on, so he did that work and I never went into the bedrooms.

On the third day he left, and after washing the breakfast dishes and sweeping the house, I went off to my classes, for the morning. Then I came back at noon and waited on table and again washed the luncheon dishes and went to classes again. When I came back in the afternoon I started to make the beds, but as I went into one of the bedrooms I found a Chinese boy at work. "What are you doing here?" I asked him and he answered, "I making bed." I said, "Why do you do that?" "Because you filed!" he announced.

I learned later on that I should not have neglected the beds until the afternoon; I should have made them in the morning, and that was the reason the Chinese boy was sent for and I was "filed." However, I watched him make up a bed and so learned how to do it.

I think I had a few cents given to me as wages for two days' work. With that in my pocket and with my bundle under my arm I looked for a job all day. Then night came. I had nowhere to go. And it was the first time in my life that I had to walk the streets all night because I had nowhere to lay my head.

In the morning I lost all patience. So with part of the money I still had, I paid for a good breakfast, and then said to myself, "I'll hang on to the rest of this money, even if I have to drop dead." In the course of my wanderings, I came to a boarding house where the landlady asked me if I could wash dishes.

I said, emphatically, "Yes!"

She asked, "Can you wait on table?"

I said, "Yes. I never spill soups."

Then she asked me, "Can you make beds?"

I answered, "Yes. I have obtained the knowledge of making beds."

"All right!" the lady said. "You can begin work this noon, my boy has left me."

This time I did everything well, so there was no cause for apprehension.

But I was beginning to feel disgruntled with my studies. For it must be remembered I had come from the University of Calcutta, where even as matriculation students we suspected the integrity of our instructors. We always felt that the instructors, being employed by the government, would only tell the truths that the government would sanction, and if I remember correctly, at that time certain books on the French Revolution were forbidden by the authorities. One of the texts that was allowed to be taught in the university was Burke's *Reflections on the French Revolution*, which, after all, was a very tame book. As I go back I recall vividly having had hot discussions with my fellow students regarding the state, society and the future of man. And a very large majority believed, with me, that professors were not allowed to teach the truth because it was dangerous. So whenever we were assigned a dangerous topic such as the French Revolution, or civil war in England under Cromwell, we read up more books on the subject than were prescribed. We did it for the purpose of contradicting the professor and finding out the truth.

I must say I missed this intellectual stimulus altogether in the American university. The undergraduate took notes as if the professor's utterances were gospel truth. There was no questioning and probing. And what astonished me most was that even if a student knew that the professor was not up to the mark, it did not enter his head to file a protest. Of course in India, protests were of no avail, but the entire student mentality in America, at that time, seemed to me to be purely apathetic. They were there to pass examinations and learn a vocation, and as long as they did that well, they did not care whether the professor was right or wrong.

One day as I was waiting on table, one young man looked up at me and said, "I see you in my class. Come up to my room and let's have a talk." Of course I had the oriental's attitude of a servant to his employer. I just bowed to him and went on waiting on table, and never let him know by even the slightest sign that I had understood. So when the meal was over he came into the kitchen, where I was eating my meal, and said: "Do you get me, that I want you to come upstairs to my room?"

And I answered, "Which room?"

He said, "You know my room."

"All right," I said, "I'll come." So when I went that evening to call on him, he received me warmly and spoke to me with a great deal of kindness.

During our talk he abruptly asked, "Do you know anything about anarchism?" I said I did and that I believed in Kropotkin's communism. With this he sneered at me and said, "That's not anarchism. That's mush."

And I asked, "What is mush?"

He replied, "The damned stuff we eat in the morning."

Of course I was perplexed, because Kropotkin in his *Conquest of Bread* never mentions mush. Leo—for that was his name—went on explaining the difference between mush and mush, and then between Kropotkin's mush and Tolstoi's mush. And he ended with a tremendous defence of Proudhon's *Anarchism* which was anti-mush. Of course I had heard of these gentlemen, though I had not read them all. Tolstoi I knew by heart, Proudhon only by name.

Leo told me to take a good look at the pictures on the walls of his room. They were, first, Adam Smith, second, Tolstoi, third, Bakunin, fourth, Kropotkin, fifth, Karl Marx, sixth, Victor Hugo, and seventh and last in the room, Jesus Christ. When he reached the last picture he said, "This man doesn't belong to a church, you ought to know that much."

And I answered, "Yes, I can quite conceive of that."

He got very excited and said, "You can conceive of that? Why, man alive, if you went with Him and showed Him the church and said it was His house He wouldn't recognize it."

I replied, "Don't you think He belongs in the very first row?"

And with a Jesuitical smile, he said, "The last shall be first."

I asked him to tell me about himself. How did he come to know about so many things which questioned the very foundation of modern society? And he began:

"I was born in an Irish family. Both my parents died in a railroad accident in Ireland. I and my two brothers were brought over to America by a maiden aunt, to live with an uncle who had made a fortune practicing law in California. My uncle brought us up. My eldest brother was trained to go into business. I was to become an Irish Catholic priest—and my third brother, who was much younger, was being trained for the bar.

"When I was young I was sent to a Jesuit school to be trained for the priesthood. There I studied Latin, French and a little Greek. They lectured on the Church fathers, and the history of the church. Gradually they built up a tremendous system before my mind, of ritual on one side, subtle thinking on the other, and both held together by the infallibility of the Pope. When I watched these Jesuit fathers trying to teach me, I realized that if people were religious they would be like them, accepting poverty and teaching the truth as they saw it.

"We were not allowed to read any books outside of our studies unless they were books bearing on the lectures. But one of the Jesuit fathers took me to his room and showed me his library and incidentally pointed out a group of books which he called agnostic writings. One book in particular attracted my attention. Its title was *Introduction to the History of Civilization in England,* by Buckle. After the father was called away and left me there alone, I took down the book and read a few pages. It gripped me so that I could not put it back. I took it to my room and read it all night.

"The next night I again burrowed into Buckle, and somewhere I came across a sentence like this: 'If there were a change in temperature and a slight dearth of oxygen in the air, the earth would be peopled by creatures entirely different from ourselves, and their conception of things would be totally different from ours.' I closed the book and I began to muse. Hitherto, I had to believe that truth was absolute, as God was absolute—nothing was relative, not even good and evil. But suppose what Buckle said was true. Then we who would be the people of that earth under different circumstances would be a different people! And our conception of God would be different, likewise of good and evil! Likewise of the infallibility of the Pope! Therefore, there is nothing absolute, I said to myself.

"I left the book in my room, walked out quite convinced that I could not accept the Absolute God when everything was truly relative, jumped over the fence of my college and disappeared into the night!"

In amazement, I asked, "What did you do? What did they do?"

Leo answered, "They notified my people. But I, who had been taught to hate the Socialists, went next morning straight to their headquarters. I did not tell them where I had come from, and they gave me Darwin and Spencer to read. I filled my mind with the Darwinian viewpoint. Page after page vanished, and I began to feel the entire structure of my belief and disbelief not only severed, but as something that had never existed. And yet, I did not know at the moment that the philosophy that was severing it had no structure either.

"To make a long story short, I began to speak from soap boxes for the Socialists on different street corners, but as I associated with them, I came to see that the majority of them had perfectly ragged minds. They did not have the finish or system of the Jesuit fathers who had taught me. They began to pall on me, for in order to overcome the system of the church, the Socialists gave me the system of social order, and that seemed even more gruesome. It had none of the sanctities, nor any of the sacerdotal superstititions which I had been accustomed to, so I threw over the whole Socialist régime and took to individualistic anarchism.

"I read Tolstoi, Kropotkin and a lot of others. This suited my temperament. It substituted 'no system' for 'system,' liberty for authority, and personality for social gregariousness.

"But you see, by this time my people had found out where I was, and what I was doing and because they were good capitalists, they became quite worried. They urged me to give up this useless life of vagabondage and study. They promised me a monthly allowance if I would go to college and study law. So here I am, trying to acquire knowledge out of the darkness in which all professors wander."

His words went to my heart, for I too was sure of the palpable darkness of the professorial night.

He asked me a lot about my country and my problems, but I knew they did not interest him. All he really wanted was to know if I would become an individualistic anarchist. There again his Jesuit training showed. He was always looking for a convert.

In the course of another week, Leo and I had become very good friends. He decided to leave the boarding house and suggested that he and I should take rooms together and live on his allowance. Instead of three meals a day, we would eat two, and the rent he paid for the room in his boarding house could easily pay for a room with two beds in a cheaper quarter. I jumped at this proposal. Not only would it bring me relief from the drudgery of dish washing, but it would also give me the companionship of a man whose ideas interested me tremendously. So we started out with our new system of housekeeping, which we called "batching."

Now began feverish hours of study. We never studied less than fourteen hours a day. We began to explore authors new to us, although familiar to others. We discovered Walt Whitman. We gave a passing glance to Bernard Shaw. We tarried at Plato's door, but found he was of the old order. Then we went on to Proudhon's *What is Property?* and were delighted with his answer, "Property is robbery." We discovered Thoreau. And last of all, out of a clear sky fell Nietzsche's thunderbolt when his *Zarathushtra* told us "God died long ago." After the latter we felt that our education was complete.

But true to the sinister working of fate, the examinations came. It caught Leo unprepared, and I only escaped by the skin of my teeth. So the next term found me alone, for Leo's people would not give him any more money to squander in studies which brought him no profit. This embittered Leo terribly and he said to me: "Now do you see the capitalistic conception of studies? If you pass your examinations you are considered intelligent. No wonder I didn't pass them." Then he took his bundle of books on his back and disappeared.

Again began for me that dreadful search for work. I rang door bells, and more door bells, but found nothing. Once in a while from nowhere, Leo would appear and call on me for he knew that the rent for our room had not as yet run out. Usually he would find me sitting on the bed trying to solve at least one problem, Hunger. He was good enough, whenever he came, either to bring a loaf of bread or a few cents. I kept myself alive on bread and water. I remember distinctly Leo giving me over my protest fifteen dollars for my college fee. "You must take it. Who knows? You might find out how capitalists manage to be what they are, and if you can get that secret, we'd break them with their own power." Here we were, existing on water and two doughnuts a day which we divided between us while we discussed the capitalist system whose fall we placed in five years! I was only nineteen years old at the time.

At last I found a job in a girls' sorority, washing dishes, taking care of the house and lawn, and waiting on table. For that, I was paid ten dollars a month and given my board. They paid me by the week! every Saturday afternoon. When the end of the week came, and I was given two dollars and a half, I felt like a king.

I remember taking a street car Sunday afternoons and meeting Leo. Usually he was standing on an inverted tub on a street corner holding forth to a crowd. I would wait until he had finished and then he would say, "My Hindu comrade will pass the hat." The hat never brought more than fifty cents and out of my week's wage I would add enough to make a complete dollar for Leo. After his speech, we would hurry to a restaurant, eat as little as possible, and talk till midnight. And often when bidding him goodnight I would beg him to come and share my room. But he would say, "No! the more I walk the streets at night the more I learn of the horrors of capitalism."

I realized for the first time that one could wear the same suit of clothes for a whole year, but the same pair of shoes are not as serviceable. My shoes were in holes by the time the rainy season in California set in. The cook in the sorority was a Negress. One day she saw me walking into the kitchen with streams of water leaking from my shoes. She said to me, "What's the matter? Hasn't you got no good shoes?"

I replied, "No, these are all I have."

"Why don't you buy some?" she asked.

And I said, "I haven't got the money to."

"You mean," she replied, "that you poor devil hasn't got no money to buy yourself a pair of shoes?"

I said, "I am no devil, but I have no money."

This was too much for her. "Think of it," she said, "that fool Clarence, my son, goes to ball games and wastes my money, and you goin' without shoes."

"Mrs. Rhodes, it's the fault of the capitalistic system."

She gave me five dollars on the spot, and said, "Go and buy a pair of shoes and then come back to work."

But I said, "I can't take your money."

"That's the fault of *your* system," she laughed and at the same time drove me out with the warning that unless I came back with a new pair of shoes I would not work in her kitchen. So I went and bought myself new shoes. Later on when I had the money to pay back, the Negress refused to take it.

As the work dragged on day after day in this girls' club house, the monotony of it all was relieved one day by the arrival of "Clarence's father." Seeing a black man standing outside the window I asked Mrs. Rhodes, the cook, who it was.

"That's Clarence's father," she replied. "I divorced him long ago. It's time for him to get some more money, so he's come."

"How much money do you give him?" I asked her.

"Oh, I don't remember," she replied, and with a smile added, "Take it from me, Gene, when you are married you'll live off a woman too."

Then Clarence's father came in and we all ate together: Clarence and Mrs. Rhodes, Mr. Rhodes, and I. Mr. Rhodes asked me where I came from. On hearing that my home was in India, he said, "Are you a Christian yet?"

"No, I am not a Christian," I confessed.

"Poor heathen," he said, "you'll never get anywhere."

Then I asked, "Mr. Rhodes, are you a Christian?"

"Christian!" he said. "I am a parson! I have passed more people into heaven than other people have prayed for. But never mind me. In your country, what do you do—worship sticks and stones?"

I said, "Yes, sticks and stones and other things besides."

He then made a very extraordinary statement: "No wonder you are a rotten people. Look at us Americans. We are the best people in the world because we are Christians."

But I remember well his taking two gold pieces from Mrs. Rhodes before he left. And she said to me, "Don't you believe a word he says, Gene. He's not a parson. He's one of them folks that stands on the street corners Sunday and shouts his head off. It does him more good than anybody else." I asked her why she had given him up. She replied, "Because he won't work and when I worked he drank with my money, and now he can't drink much, so he talks every Sunday. Look here, Gene," she added, "if you ever need money, don't forget me. I never seen a fellow so nice as you. You work all the time. Do you think you've got any brains?"

"I don't know," I said, and evidently neither did she for she shook her head dubiously.

II

My Socialist "Friends"

Time passed, and the spring examinations were coming. Leo began to visit me more frequently and to borrow books, through me, from the university library. I borrowed and gave him Hegel to read. Then he went back to Aristotle, and then he borrowed Schopenhauer. Leo was now able to give a lucid statement of Hegel's philosophy and I know that he never had more than one meal a day during this entire period. Once I said so to him, and he answered me: "A full stomach is opposed to philosophy. Thank God I can starve."

When the summer vacation came, I left the university and went to San Francisco to find a job. Leo, who went with me, vowed that he would never work again. "Why should I work and enrich the capitalist system?" he asked.

"But somebody's got to work," I insisted, to which his only answer was: "Well, you go to work, if you like."

"I'll have to," I said, and so I found an all-day job in a boarding house taking care of thirty people, waiting on table, washing dishes, making beds, and answering the telephone. The work took ten hours a day, but it left my evenings free. For this I received twenty dollars a month, including room and board. Every evening I would go and meet Leo and he would give me the résumé of a chapter of the book he had read.

While in this last place, I came across a very strange form of stupid cupidity. The landlady, who rented out rooms, had an enormous family of her own. Her husband didn't work; her sons didn't work. One of her sons never came home sober. She had three daughters, one of whom was married and living there with her family. So it seemed to me out of the thirty paying guests that she had, this poor landlady was supporting thirty guests that never paid—her own children and their descendents. The men seemed utterly callous. You could always find one of them loafing about doing nothing. The telephone could be ringing on and on, and they would never even answer it. Their father was a perfect ruffian, always quarreling and shouting. Their mother seemed like a saint but one who tried to make money out of everything, counting every penny to earn enough to support this horde of dependents.

What annoyed me most was the way her daughters used to flirt with her paying guests, and in the course of time I discovered that that was one of the reasons why the paying guests stayed on. Underneath it all, I found out that the daughters did not enjoy doing this sort of thing, but they had to do it in order to support their enormous family.

They exploited everybody who worked for them. Any time the servants wanted to take a vacation, they had to pay fifty cents an hour out of their wages. I used to find at the end of the month that five dollars out of my twenty dollars had gone, deducted for the laundry, deducted for time off, deducted for broken plates. Every apron that I wore, and every white jacket that I was made to wear when waiting on table, was deducted out of my wages. With this steady practice of petit larceny I began to see the capitalist system soaring upwards and reaching its apex in the head of that old woman.

But it left me my evenings to myself. That was the advantage of this employment.

One evening Leo came and asked me to go and meet a well-known anarchist, whom I will call Jerry. Jerry had been held up to me as the ideal anarchist. So I felt extremely confused at the prospect of meeting him.

As I was arranging my necktie, Leo said, "Bah, if you wear a white collar, Jerry will never shake hands with you."

"But you can't go through the streets without a collar!" I exclaimed.

"You see what a bourgeois you are," replied Leo. "The capitalist system has implanted in your soul what it demands from everyone. You are a slave. You've got the slave psychology." We sauntered out, without collars, and came to a place called the "pinochle joint" where in the back room we found a gray-haired man reading by a lamp.

Hearing our footsteps, he stood up and stretched out his hand to me and said, "How do you do? I am Jerry." I was extremely embarrassed and nervous at meeting this man of whom I had heard so many splendid things. I vividly recall the power of his paw with which he shook my hand, and then as I drank the whiskey, almost the first I had ever tasted, which Jerry offered, I felt as proud as any anarchist that ever threw a bomb. I gave him back his flask, which he emptied, and we all sat down.

Jerry asked, "What makes you so interested in anarchism?"

I replied, "Why, it's the vision of the future." "That shows you know nothing about it," laughed Jerry. "Vision of the future! That's a bourgeois phraseology. They tell that in every church, every Sunday. You are not an anarchist. An anarchist never uses phrases that are grandiose. By the way, why don't you go back to India? Your ancestors found the truths you are seeking thousands of years ago; Buddha was the greatest of all anarchists."

"But you, surely, don't believe in God, do you?" I asked very much astonished.

"Why not? God is nothing but a phantasm as I am a phantasm myself," Jerry replied. "It is good to hail a brother phantasm anywhere."

"But," I said, "Jerry, you are an anarchist."

He answered, "Yes, if spending twenty-seven years of your life without doing a stroke of work makes one an anarchist, then I am the only anarchist that exists. I have not worked for the last twenty-seven years, because I was present at the 'Haymarket' in Chicago. You remember when that bomb was thrown, because the police beat up the crowds. What was it about? Those poor people were agitating for eight hours a day. I was there on the spot. I saw the policeman charge with their sticks. And then out of the terrible welter of humanity came a fierce, an awful noise that made everybody stand still, policeman and crowds alike. The world shook for a moment. And that convinced me."

"Of what? Didn't you have any philosophical background or anything?" I asked him.

"No," said he, "that explosion was my background. And now I pray to myself, 'Let it be my foreground as well!'" Jerry rose before me like a god, a sort of Triton from the deeps—an explosion before him and an explosion behind him.

I said, "What did you do?"

"I never did a stroke of work since, and I vowed to myself that I'd never help the capitalist system with the slightest exertion of a single muscle."

I could not understand. "How do you live?" I asked.

"Why, people give me food," he said. "You call it charity, why not? If you are an anarchist there is no pride nor humility for you, no matter what happens."

And I asked, "Do people give you enough?"

"Oh, yes!" Jerry said. "Man is a strange slave. If he is not the slave of love, he is indeed the slave of pity. If you arouse his pity he'll do anything for you. I seem to do nothing but arouse everybody's pity. I despise them for it. I am nothing but an occasion on which they exploit their own emotion. I continually feel like a victim."

I put another question to him. "Yet, do you believe in a better future for humanity when you despise mankind?"

His response was typical, "I despise the common herd, but I cannot despise the individual man. Whenever he stoops to pity I think of the common herd, but whenever he flays me with his insolence I think of the individual man."

I exclaimed, "Jerry, I'll give up everything and go with you and study under you!"

He said, "No. You couldn't stand it."

"But why not?" I asked.

"It is terrible," he replied, "to be beaten in prison, to be kicked, and then sometimes given a good dinner. You couldn't endure it twenty-seven years. In your country you have exalted beggary by making it a religious affair, but in our country we have reduced beggary to such a crime that even thieves think they are disgraced if they beg. You cannot do it. To you begging is a religious ritual. You can't beg in the West. No."

I asked him if he had been to India.

"No," he admitted, "but one can fathom India. I can feel them, those old Hindus. Once in a while I have read a scrap of their writings, and I have felt then that they were the primordial anarchists. Isn't it one of your ancestors who said, 'This world is not, is not, is not'?" I admitted this. "Then," he barked at me: "Why in hell do you want to be an anarchist? I am an anarchist because I am a leader. I am not an anarchist because I am an example."

"What do you lead us into?" I asked him.

"Into a greater sense of social danger," he replied. "I want to lead you from security to bravery."

I bade him good-night and went to my little hole to sleep. I met him again the next day, and we had more discussion. I was still clinging to my belief that through anarchism, humanity might come to better things, still believing that environment creates character, so that if we did change environment, the world would be better. I asked Jerry, "Do you really believe that man comes from the monkeys, as Darwin says?"

And he answered, "That's nothing. What frightens me is that man is going back so fast to the monkeys."

"Isn't civilization adaptation?" I asked. There was a Socialist, Gordon, present who thought that it was Spencer who had said this.

Jerry said, "Who is Spencer, anyway? If Gordon quotes him, there is nothing in it."

Gordon got furious and argued. He was one of those sticklers who make a point of pointlessness. "If you want to win a point I'll make you a present of it," was all he could get out of Jerry.

Gordon repeated, "Civilization is adaptation."

"No," said Jerry. "Let me tell you a story."

"One of Mukerji's ancestors came to a river one day when it was running fierce and full. He bowed to it and said, 'O Mother Ganges, I must adapt myself to your beauty and wrath!' I suppose you would explain this old Hindu's behavior as adaptation. The river flooded his hut, and he built another. He kept on adapting himself. But this old Hindu's great-great-great-grandson saw one day a log on the water. That gave the great-great-great-grandson a new idea: he tied six or seven logs together, made a raft and crossed the river. He, you will say, started civilization. I agree with you. But would you call it adaptation? No. Its real name is exploitation. This man exploited the water. Civilization is exploitation and not adaptation. Your Spencer man is wrong."

"Bah! Oriental stories," was Gordon's comment. "You may convince an Easterner like Mukerji. After all he's a damn fool. But I want logic."

And Jerry said, "Mythology is the logic of imaginative races, as logic is the mythology of the dull races." Gordon left us, furious.

I said to Jerry, "Do you believe that Gordon might be right?"

He answered, "The curse of these Socialists is that they are always right. They haven't the courage to be wrong. But let us forget Gordon."

And Jerry added: "They are always barking and howling and clamoring. They don't realize that the thing is too deep. A system of doubt will never overcome a system of belief."

I must say that Jerry and Leo were not earning a penny, and it was time I got my twenty dollars. With five dollars deducted from it, I did not feel inclined to give them five dollars, and yet I felt bound to do so, because they were improving my mind. All day they studied and at night they would tell me what they had studied. Thus they took me across Hegel and Hume. They also took me across what are called the thick and thin kinds of social theories.

One day when I came with my salary of fifteen dollars in my pocket, Leo said: "Dhan, we've got a job and we're going to take it. We are going to lecture for the I.W.W. They are the only branch of Socialists we can support. They are going to give us as compensation the floor of their hall to sleep on. Jerry and I won't have to sleep on the streets any more, and sleeping in box cars is tiresome."

I asked, "What do you do in exchange?"

"We are supposed to speak twice a week on a street corner," Leo answered, adding, "Do you mind carrying the soap box for us?"

I said, "No. I will gladly contribute that much. We must destroy the capitalist system. My carrying the box is another stroke of the pick at the foundation of capitalism."

Soon the first evening's lecture began. I had borrowed an apple box from my employer's house, and carried it way up there to Fillmore Street. I took it on a street car, and the passengers thought I was carrying a cat in it. Then when they saw an empty box they looked at me, as much as to say that my mind was as empty as the box. At last I reached my destination and put the box down. Leo stood on it and said: "I want to abolish the State and the Church and Society." That fetched only one man as audience. And I said to myself, "if he has abolished those three and got only one man, what else can he abolish to get some more? There is very little left."

The audience said to Leo: "Say, what are you?"

Leo answered, "I am an anarchist."

The audience said, "I get you. Go to it."

"What's the use of going to it?" responded Leo. "Get about five more people."

Our one convert agreed to this. "Take my advice," he added, "don't talk. Let us stand around a while." So we waited and watched Leo who stood on the box firm as a statue. This ruse had a tremendous effect. It brought a lot of people. Then Leo flung out an arm at them and pointed with his finger and cried: "You are the people who support the State, the Church and Society." And these people grew interested and frightened!

Then Leo launched into his speech. And as he went on the crowd became more and more interested. He talked for more than two hours. Then with a great gesture Leo said, "Now my Hindu comrade will pass the hat." I could see a swaying movement in the crowd. The greater part of it melted into the night. Those who remained gave us a dollar and a half. Then Leo announced: "The collection is quite satisfactory. I hope I shall meet you next Monday night, when my comrade Jerry will address you on the abolition of marriage."

But before the week was out many things happened. The most important in its consequences was that my employer said to me one evening: "Do you mind staying in and answering the 'phone? We are going out on very important business." So I stayed in and answered the telephone that evening. The next two evenings the same request was made, and I gave the same answer. In the course of the week, it was taken for granted that it was part of my job to answer the telephone in the evening. I was loath to give up this position because it was not a very bad one, and as long as I had my evenings there was some compensation. Now they were making it absolutely impossible for me to attend the evening conferences with Leo and Jerry after the day's work.

I reported this fact one evening to Jerry. He said, "You must stick to this job for none of us is earning anything." I replied, "But I am tired of being exploited."

"Well, then, give it up," Jerry said, "I don't care. But take my advice: save money."

I was quite worried, so one evening when the woman announced, "We are going on very important business, please answer the 'phone," I said, "No. I have a very important engagement and I must keep it. I cannot do it. I must go."

"If that's the case, out of this house for good you go tomorrow!" she stated.

I clung to my determination. "All right," I said, "I'll be willing to leave tonight." I went out and met the boys and we had a lively discussion on "What is the relation of man to society?"

Jerry said, "The basis of the relation of man to society is fear." Leo maintained, "The basis of the relation is ignorance. The more you know the more unsocial you are."

Then I realized that man's relation to society was something neither of them knew anything about! I had just come away from that woman's wrath and I knew my relation to her was very delicate, because I wanted to preserve my job. I told Jerry what had happened. He said, "You'll keep your job tomorrow. They won't fire you. No one will ever find a perfectly pliable fool like you. You have too damned much non-resistance in you. That's what's the matter with you."

I went home that night and as I lay asleep I heard someone banging at my door. I woke up and heard furious swearing accompanied with more poundings. I was very much frightened but soon found out what it was. My employer had told her drunken son that I refused to answer the telephone. He came home and wanted to throw me out, and he raged all night but could not get at me. When in the morning I opened my door I found him on the floor in front of my room fast asleep. I went up and called the old woman to help; then we put him to bed, and as he was going to sleep after a few wakeful moments, he said, "You damned heathen, I will smash your head!" With that he fell asleep.

I told the old woman I must leave because I had been insulted. "Your son raged at my door, and called me a damned heathen," I explained.

"I don't call that an insult," she protested.

"What do you call an insult, then?" I asked.

"If he had hit you, I would call it an insult," she said.

I left that job. I couldn't wait to be hit.

Now began the most difficult part of my life. I could not find a job at once. We were allowed to sleep on the floor of the I.W.W. place, but the boys had to make four speeches a week for the privilege, and as Leo said, "No man can make four speeches a week without being a perfect humbug." So it came about, that whenever they needed to make a speech, I was made to carry the box. Any time that any of the group felt inclined to deliver himself of a course on the abolishment of the Church or marriage, he always looked for Mukerji, because he was associated with the box. Then there came a quarrel as to policy between the I.W.W. and Jerry. Jerry insisted that even industrial control should not be in the hands of the workers, because that would be a violation of individualism, and the I.W.W. said he must always insist in his speeches on industrial control by the workers. As Jerry refused, the I.W.W. people declared, "Then you don't sleep here."

"All the better," said Jerry, "I'll be rid of your vermin."

They said, "All right. We'll keep our vermin. You get out!"

So we left, all three of us. And we made a present of the box to them because we did not need to make any more speeches for a sleeping place.

Walking the streets at night, instead of sleeping, has its disadvantages. Of course we slept all day long in the park. It was summer time in California; there was no rain. But the stupidity of policemen is unfathomable. They were always accusing us of something or other, and their monotonous motto was: "Move on!"

One day Jerry thought he would placate a park policeman by talking to him of Irish nationalism, of the Phoenix Park tragedy, and of Parnell. From that time on the policeman was our friend, and two benches under the bushes became our sleeping quarters undisturbed by any one of those who used to chase us away.

Eating was more precarious than sleeping. We would run errands for people—that is to say, I ran the errands and Leo and Jerry sat on the benches and studied. I took the job of looking after a book shop. This was a Socialist book shop where I dusted old books upstairs and made a record of them. It was three hours' work a day, but the Socialists I found very stingy people who would not give me more than twenty-five cents an hour. Whenever I made seventy-five cents I would not work any more but we would all go and eat a meal.

One day Jerry said, "You know, lack of food undermines one's system. One of us must go to work." So I went and found a job. This time it was twenty-five dollars a month, room and board, and the same sort of work I had done before, so I had no difficulty. But the place was rather shady. There were a number of suspicious-looking people, coming and going, and no one stayed more than a week. So after I had my first week's wages I took them over to Jerry and Leo and told them the nature of the place. "The more suspicious it is, the better," they said. "That means that people won't demand very good service, and you'll have more time and tips. Some of these people are loose. And you know it is the loose that are generous."

They were right. There was much less fastidiousness, and less economy. People did not mind tipping and did not mind if I neglected certain things. The person there most interesting to me was a widow who lived on her own income. She was the only one who stayed there all the time. One day I saw her reading Locke's *On Human Understanding* at breakfast. Unable to restrain myself, I said, "Do you understand Locke?"

"How dare you!" she exclaimed, evidently very angry.

"But Madame," I tried to quiet her, "Jerry tells me it's a profound book." In spite of this bad start I had many pleasant talks with her and added to my store of knowledge.

One day I said to her, "Do you believe in abolishing marriage?"

"In my case I have abolished it," she replied. "I am not a widow. I am a divorced woman."

This was the first time in my life that I had come across a real divorced person and I did not know what to make of her. "How does it feel to be divorced?" I asked.

"You feel well rid," she answered. "Rid of what, you ask? Well, I cannot explain to you, but I'll tell you: Never live a lie!"

"It must be the fault of the capitalist system that people live lies," I told her, true to my teaching.

"All right, have it your own way," she agreed, and then added, "Have you ever read *Ghosts,* by Ibsen? In *Ghosts* a woman lived a lie for many years."

This started me reading Ibsen, and I found that the connection between *The Doll's House* and *Ghosts* was perfect. And what convinced me of Ibsen's greatness was the fact that this woman had lived and verified Ibsen's theory.

When I told Jerry about my new friend and Ibsen he protested that Ibsen was a back number. As he put it, "Ibsen isn't quite sure of anything. He questioned and questioned and questioned, and pretty soon he wasn't sure of his questioning even. But since Sophocles no one has written with such simplicity."

The next day we took down Sophocles and began to read him. When we had finished in two or three days, Jerry asked, "Do you see now that Shakespeare was a ranting fool compared to this man?"

"What's wrong with Shakespeare?"

"There's nothing wrong with him, except that he had the tremendous belief that two worlds could be kept up by the same man. He compromised with the earth as well as with heaven. Shakespeare accepted the order of this world and he also accepted the order of the inner world. He never found out that both needed simplification, but in Sophocles the two are brought into a unity."

I asked him again about Ibsen. He said, "Ibsen, if he had had a higher medium like the Greek language and contemporaries like Socrates and Pericles, would have been just as great. But the trouble with Ibsen is that his contemporaries were men like Gladstone. But, Mukerji, your ancestors knew all this and never were troubled about it. It is strange that you should come to us to find out what you had at home. It's time for you to go back."

It *was* time for me to go back to college. Vacation was over.

III

The Second Year in College

When I came back to the university, life seemed extremely flat. There was the same dull monotony of study, and the routine of lectures. Not that the lectures were necessarily shallow, but somehow I did not want to listen to the wisdom of my masters.

Leo used to come and see me once in a while, and so did Jerry. It was toward the end of the semester that the real importance of college life began to emerge. I felt that the only thing university life could give a young man was a love of books. Yet the wisdom to implant a love of the real books is not within the power of a professor to give but is an acquirement that a student must seek out for himself. Out of every ten books that I read only one was of any value to me, and as I blundered through book after book I at last attained a sense of certainty about them. I did have to blunder through ten books to find the one. Then my taste for reading left me. All books seemed to wear the same stupid expression. Each one looked as bald and spectacled as its neighbor—very much like a series of college professors preserved in mummy cases.

It was very fortunate that that semester exhausted all my love for the dead. One day Jerry and Leo came to see me. At this time I was working in a boarding house for room and board and ten dollars a month. Whenever the boys wanted to see me, they came to my room in the basement and we had long talks. I told Jerry what had happened to me. I said, "The books have died."

Jerry replied, "Books are the reflections of great characters. When a young mind acquires the power to discern the character of man, he will cease to be interested in books. Books are shadows and it requires sufficient youth to be in love with shadows."

"But there are great books like those of Shakespeare and Sophocles," I protested.

"Oh, yes," he admitted, "but today I could no more love a play of Shakespeare's than I could love a mountain. It seems so heavy and unnecessary. On the contrary the man, Shakespeare, gives one's mind a spacing which nothing else can give. Books are dead when you have attained the psychic qualities of knowing them without knowing their contents."

"But there is one thing about books; they help us forget life," Leo assented.

"Yes," agreed Jerry, "books are opium. The Chinese take it by the lump and we have it spread out on paper. It has the same effect on our minds in the alphabetical order as when taken in lumps."

Then I answered, "I am going to give up college."

"No, stick to it," Jerry urged, "for some day the human race will become alive and because these strongholds will fight for the dead, for the sake of the living we will have to destroy them. Those who know their secrets are the ones that shall be needed at that hour."

I was now feeling hungry and proposed that the three of us should dine on the dollar that I had in my pocket, for I knew that I was a dollar richer than my two friends. So we went to a restaurant, and as we were eating, in walked a man, his face covered with a golden beard and his head thick with a beautiful mane. "How do you do, Jerry?" he said, coming up to our table.

Jerry turned around and said, "Hello, Frank! I thought you were in jail in Australia."

"No," said Frank, "They didn't catch me and as I am a political offender, they cannot take me here." Jerry then introduced him to us. His name was Frank Bonnington.

Bonnington said, "Is this a meal in which everyone can join?"

Jerry answered, "Ask Mukerji, because he is the one who has the power."

"Ninety cents are gone," I said, "but you may get what you can with ten cents."

"That means a lot to me," replied Frank. "I haven't eaten a thing for three days."

"What happened to you in Australia?" I asked.

"Oh, I led two syndicalist strikes and put a factory 'on the blink.' Then a guard had a warrant against me, but I got wind of it and stowed away in an American boat. I left Sydney a month ago. When they found me I had already starved three days, but they gave be some work to do and let me land in San Francisco. I thought that the Socialist movement was so rampant in America that a man could find his comrades anywhere."

Jerry said, "That's just what's the trouble with the Socialist movement here. There are as many Socialists in America as there are fleas on a dog!"

I asked Frank whether he had any extraordinary experience in the course of his work. "No," he said, "my skull was broken in two places once and another time I had to stand all alone keeping watch over a group of women and children, whose husbands had been arrested. The most terrible part of it all was that the children cried for milk and the women cried for food and I had nothing to give them. The only thing that tided us over was the singing. We sang the 'Marseillaise' so that in the delirium of it we forgot everything about hunger."

"But how can you think with a broken skull?" asked Jerry.

To this Frank said, "I have never been more lucid than now. I wish your skull was broken in three places, then you could think much better."

"It is not the broken skull that I am objecting to," Jerry said, "but how can you think lucidly when you are a Socialist? No Socialist thinks clearly, he thinks emphatically."

Frank then told us that he had a job at eighty dollars a month editing a Socialist weekly. "Well, that will keep us all going, I think," Jerry said, and then he pointed at me. "Look here, Frank, this fellow wants to give up college and go hoboing with us, but I don't think he is fit for it." Whether or not I was fit to be a hobo, I assured them I was not going back to college as I had found the life there altogether flat, and I wanted to give my life to humanity. To this Frank answered, "All life is flat; even getting your skull broken, if done often enough, is very tiresome. And as for giving your life to humanity, humanity has heard that sentence so often from young men that she does not care to answer whether she wants it or not! Why do you want to crucify humanity always by giving it your life?"

"But have you not given your life to humanity?" I asked him.

"No," said Frank, "I give my life to a dream that I pursue. I was born a gentleman—my grandfather was a slave owner, my father fought in the Civil War to preserve the slaves that we owned. After the war I was sent to the University of Virginia to be a gentleman and after spending four years there, I found out it was the one thing I did not want to be. So I left the East and walked west to California. I have been kicked out of restaurants for eating without paying for food; I have been locked up in different police stations as a suspected thief; I have eaten food out of garbage cans; I have slept beneath the stars under the Allegheny mountains as well as the Rockies, and let me tell you, I had no desire to love humanity. I had no desire to do good; I had no desire even to improve myself. But a sudden vision seized me and compelled me to believe that a higher social order is essential for the growth of the free spirit. I believe that there will be a dissolution of church, state and society in a higher human organism. I believe in freedom so heartily that I am enslaved to my dream of freedom."

Here the talk drifted into diverse channels, mostly about books to read and people to know and finally ended with a discussion on Nietzsche. All agreed that Nietzsche was looking for the morally strong man and that in order to make clear to his contemporaries what he meant by the moral man and the strong man he was so vehement that people mistook his vehemence for his truth.

Jerry ended by saying, "Oh, well, he was a dreary windbag. If you are really strong men you have never served yourself to your fullest, and if you are immoral men, you have clean forgotten what is good or bad. An instance of that is the German who goes and dances all over Europe telling us that the morally strong man is himself. The result is Europe thinks he is not immoral but weak."

"But what would happen to humanity if we all took a stand like that?" I asked.

Jerry said, "Humanity! What about your ancestors? They sat in the Indian jungle and meditated while tigers came, elephants went and the crocodiles bobbed up and then sank down again in the Ganges. But these Indians did not care. They would pursue a truth which was larger than humanity—larger than themselves and so they could forget to be annihilated by the truth of pursuit. The trouble with us is that we have such small lives and such small truths. We are like very sanitary pig-stys open for inspection as if there were a royal visit on. This humanity that you talk of is a thing you know nothing about. A million human hearts beat, but how many have you counted? Of thousands and thousands of years, how many have you dared to look into? And those terrible sufferings that are all hidden from our vision? How few have we dared to cure! And then we sit here and want to give our life to humanity. We want to die martyrs to truth. I hate the word, martyrdom! It smacks so of charity! Do not be charitable to humanity. It is so unkind."

"Well," I said, "I want to tell you something very frankly. I am going to lose my job. They want to save money so they are going to fire me anyway, but what is the use of going to school?"

"How much money does it cost you to go to school?" Frank asked.

"Forty dollars a month," I answered.

"All right," said Frank, "I will give you half of my salary and you go to school on that while with the other forty I will take care of Leo, Jerry and myself."

I was staggered by this proposition and in consternation I said, "Why do you do this? I do not need schooling. Look how much you know without depending on a college professor."

But Frank would not abandon his plan for my education in favor of his own. "Colleges are far kinder than anything or any place else," he said. "They give you knowledge without hurting you. On the other hand bumming around is the stiffest way of acquiring wisdom. It hurts you most; for it destroys your self-respect. Do you know, many times after going without food for days, and being unable to bear it any longer I have gone to a restaurant and ordered a meal. Naturally they would ask me to pay for it at the end. Well you know the rest." Frank waved his hand.

"What do you mean by the rest?" I asked.

Frank shrugged his shoulders and explained, "I offered myself to be kicked out of the restaurant; which they did with great alacrity. . . Now you see what it means to be a hobo? It means that you lose your greatest asset—you have no faith in anything, even in your own greatness."

"How do you endure life under such trials?" I questioned.

"You put all of your life out of yourself," he answered. "You think and live in a far future when man will be as the Titans. Since you live in the far off, you don't mind the here and the now. Your intellect weaves a splendid mantle of self-delusion which armors your ego."

"Well," said Jerry, "what is intellect for if it is not for the purpose of hypnotizing us into believing that the position we are in is the highest and most envied by all?"

"However that may be," Frank closed the argument, "you must go to school and leave the expenses to me." So I dragged through another semester at college. When vacation came, I went to San Francisco and took a job. It was full day's work for room, board and twenty-five dollars a month. It was pleasant to feel that I was working there to save up money for college and also to pay back Frank.

One day, after my day's work, as I went to a little cigar store where we all were in the habit of meeting, I found a huge crowd talking very anxiously in whispers. I found out that they had received news that Emma Goldman and Riteman had been in San Diego where they were tarred and feathered. All the radicals were so excited! What was to be done! Well, I sought out our group. Jerry said, "This is the most lively news in a decade, for at last they have consented to take notice of anarchists. What an advertisement for the cause! How fortunate!"

"Jerry, does it feel awful to be tarred and feathered?" I asked.

"I do not know," he answered. "My devotion to anarchism never went to that length."

"What are we going to do?" I asked.

"Well, the situation is very difficult," he said. "There are the MacNamara brothers who are being tried in Los Angeles for having blown up the Times Building and killed so many people. Here are Emma and Riteman in a scrape. Now reading the thing from the standpoint of the bourgeoisie of Los Angeles, tarring and feathering is a pretty mild form of punishment. But these people are our comrades, so I do not know what to do."

"Jerry," Frank said, "you ought to go down to San Diego at once and help poor Emma. It is a rotten trick to play on a woman."

"There you go," Jerry said, "always conventional. When did anarchists ever recognize barriers of sex? A male anarchist is just as good as a female. There is no difference."

"Well, are you going to go down and help them?" asked Frank.

Jerry said, "Yes, I will."

So the next day Jerry set out. When he reached San Diego, matters had been straightened out, so he decided to go to Los Angeles. He went to the court room where the MacNamara brothers were being tried and there he met his brother, who was one of the lawyers interested in the case. The next day we received the following letter from him:

Dear Leo

I have found my brother. That is to say he has found me. He is a lawyer. He is just as bad a character as my other brother who is a real estate agent and when he saw me in the court room he let everyone know that I was his brother, which was extremely disconcerting since we had not seen each other for sixteen years. There is something very embarrassing in being called a brother by a man whose ideals are alien to you. And the most embarrassing thing happened when he gave me $100.00 to buy clean clothes and good shoes in order to take me with him to Chicago for a family reunion. Will you please send me a copy of Stierner's

Ego and His Own, and Nietzsche's *Beyond Good and Evil?*
The bourgeois hounds are after me. For God's sake, save me.
I need the books badly.

Leo and I re-read the letter and wondered what to do for Jerry. Leo said, "We have no money—at least he has that and what is the use of sending him books? We have only two books left and if we send him both, where would we be? If he has met his brother—well, after all, a fellow ought to have some family experience anyway!"

"But," I said, "his family will gobble him up and that will make him a bourgeois."

Leo said, "Jerry has not worked for twenty-five years. You cannot destroy twenty-five years of inactivity by a trip to Chicago. Jerry is the solidest anarchist we have."

Leo was right. In three days Jerry appeared—his pockets bulging with money. He said, "Now we are sure of a good homestead for the next five or six months at least. I am going to rent a room for all of us so that anyone of us who wants to sleep will have a place in which to sleep. There are three of us—twenty-four hours—so each one can sleep eight hours. Let us go and find a room." Jerry added, "Now, Mukerji, you can give up your job and come over here and we will all study together as long as the money holds out. When all the money is gone, we will again disperse and each go his separate way." So I went to my employer and gave him notice that I would leave at the end of the week. This was the first time I had resigned before being discharged and I felt very proud.

We got together in the evening of the following day and began to discuss all sorts of things. It was the first time that Jerry told us the secret of his life. He said, "We were six children in our family with an ailing mother and with an erratic father forced to emigrate to America from Ireland. My mother died in the basement of a tenement house in New York when I was ten years old. We did not go to school for fear that the day would be wasted, so we worked as errand boys or newsboys to make money to support our three sisters. Well, our father sometimes got a job and sometimes did not and once in a while he would come home and beat us all to relieve his nerves. One day one of the girls was sick. And among us all we had just twenty-eight cents. The rent was due. We hoped and prayed that our father would bring at least ten dollars home that night.

"He came home at nine o'clock reeking with the smell of whiskey. He was quite drunk. We asked him about the money that we expected.

Our questions maddened him so that without the slightest warning he hit my eldest brother in the face. Then he hit the second one. As if that had urged him on to do something more brutal yet, he began to beat the girl who was sick in bed. Unable to bear it any longer, though frightened almost to death, with a sudden and desperate courage I attacked him. His blows fell all over me. But I clung and tore at his neck. Then like a bulldog I fastened on his throat with my teeth. He hit me again and again to make me loosen my hold. But I would not let go. I was afraid to, for I knew that once freed from his pain he would waste no time in catching me. Then suddenly I felt a strange taste in my mouth. My father groaned most pitifully. I felt so sick—now that I had tasted blood. So I let go not caring for the consequences. My father reeled back, then fell. I waited for his next attack. But he lay on the ground and moaned. My heart grew heavy. Now that I saw my brothers and sisters crouching in dread and terror in the corner of the room I felt sick in my soul

"I walked out into the night. . . I wandered through New York. At daybreak I returned home. The children were fast asleep, but my father's bed was empty, and I could not find him anywhere in the house. My brothers and my sick sister were roused by the noise I made in my search. They told me that father went out right after I left the house. They could tell me nothing more about him. Even to this day no one knows where he disappeared to.

"His going away like that put the burden of supporting the family full on the shoulders of us boys. And I must say we did it very well for the following two years."

"What happened then?" asked Leo.

Jerry answered, "The thing that settled my destiny. One day as I was coming home from work I saw a lot of people walking in a parade. They were an awfully ragged-looking lot. They were a bunch of unemployed. It was raining like anything and yet they walked on. I went home and talked to my brothers but they just laughed at the matter and said, 'if they are out of employment, it's their own fault. The trouble with these people is they do not want to work. No wonder they are unemployed.' I left the house and walked back toward the park. It took one hour and a quarter to walk there. The rain was pouring and I was sopping wet. I found men and women standing under doorways, their clothes all wet and their eyes green with hunger. For the first time I realized that hunger is a universal fact. Mankind experiences more truth through hunger than through anything else. When I went back home it was midnight. I hung up my clothes and went to bed. Next day I did not go to work.

"I must tell you a little about my brothers. They were not only working wonderfully but they were going to night school and bettering themselves all the time. One of them had set his heart on law as his vocation and the other had not decided on anything so he was taking a business course. We really had enough money to take care of the girls, so after seeing them employed I stopped going to work. I cursed everything and then after that an emptiness set in that I could not control. I sat in an empty house waiting for the girls to come back from school and the boys from work. I had dinner ready for them. They could not understand me when I told them why I had not gone to work. The emptiness began to grow apace. Again I walked out into the night and watched for the unemployed, who were looking for shelter in all kinds of strange places. All night I walked. When the day broke, I could not go home.

"Then began my vagabondage. In the course of my wandering I heard all kinds of tales about distribution of wealth, and increase in production; but the only man that ever gripped my imagination was a fellow called Emerson, whose *Conduct of Life* fell to my hands. Queer bird, Emerson! He lived through the Civil War. There is very little mention of this fact in his journals. For the first time in my life I came across a man who could live through a war and yet not be touched by it. I read all the journals and everything written by this man. Today the thing that I remember is that slight phrase: somewhere, he has said, 'We must be counted singly, individually, alone.' He made me an individualist.

"Within a year or so I went to Chicago and was present at that parade at Haymarket where the bomb exploded. The first counterstroke of labor against capital! Then I walked from Chicago to New York, all the time devouring more of Emerson. I came home and stayed there to work in a factory and study in a library, but the thing that bewildered me most was this: my sister who was brought up in poverty was now in love with a young man who gave her expensive presents. My brothers, who were poor, were now branching out into rich vocations and there was I, a factory laborer yet.

"Suddenly this truth dawned on me—that environment does not shape a man's nature. Here was my sister brought up in the same environment as my brothers and I. They had all gone in for wealth and here was I yet wondering as to the meaning and the nature of the universe. I concluded that we are not determined by our environment, but we are determined by our character. There is no such thing as a material determinism but there is the primordial truth of psychological determinism. Was it Emerson who told me this or was it life?"

IV

Something of Frank's Life

A t the end of his story of his boyhood, Jerry got up impatiently and
said: "Now let us go and find a room." After a short search from
place to place, we came across a nice landlady who rented us a room for
six months. Jerry asked her: "Do you mind if three people sleep in the
same bed?"

"What do you mean, sir?" the landlady said.

Jerry repeated, "May three people sleep in the same bed?"

She said, "Do you mean man, woman and baby, sir?"

"No," said Jerry, "I mean one man the first eight hours, another man
the second eight hours, and a third man, the rest of the time. Can they
sleep in the same bed? Do you have any objections if three people sleep
in the same bed successively?"

The landlady at last understood our proposal and said, "I do not care
who sleeps in the bed as long as the rent is paid."

Jerry then took out a roll of money from his pocket and said, "Here
is money for three months' rent. Is that enough?"

She nodded as she counted the money and the three of us filed out
of the rooming-house. When we came out to the park bench where
we had spent many nights, we were rather perplexed as to who was
to begin sleeping in our common bed. After a great deal of debate it
was decided to cast lots. After we tossed up we found that Leo was to
sleep first, either Frank or myself the second eight hours, depending on
which was out of employment, and last it was for Jerry to go to sleep.

Jerry, however, said, "This looks like a regular bourgeois arrangement,
everything according to law and order. I won't abide by it. Are we to lose
our freedom because we have rented a room? We will sleep whenever
we please, that is all."

Then we went to a restaurant and ate our meal. I went on to my own
place where I had been working, to spend the night and I did not see
the boys for several days.

It was the fourth night while I was just getting into bed that I
heard someone scratch the windowpane of my basement room. I was
frightened, but after a few moments I realized that it was one of the

comrades. So I went outside and found Leo. When I had brought him in, he said, "Will you let me sleep with you tonight?"

I said, "What's the matter?"

He explained, "Well, Frank is there to sleep in that bed and Jerry wanted to sleep, too, though his turn hadn't yet come. So what could I do? Frank has come out from the other side of the Bay and there was Jerry and me. The three of us wanted to sleep, so I left the two other fellows there. Now, if you will let me get into bed. . ."

The next night Frank was sent to me to sleep in my bed while Leo was to sleep in Jerry's bed in the rented room. After we had been in bed a few moments, Frank said, "What the devil is that biting me? Has anyone else been here besides Leo?"

"No," I answered.

"Do you know what I think?" he said after a little, "I think that the place we rented is full of vermin and Leo has brought all the vermin from there to here and I have brought some of my own since I slept there. However, if we have stood the capitalist system these many years we can stand the vermin one night."

So we slept and scratched and slept and scratched again.

Early next morning Frank departed to give up the room and to give that vulture of an old woman a piece of his mind. Hardly had he stepped out of the back door when he came back with Leo in a great hurry. "Something terrible has happened," Leo said. "Jerry has been arrested."

"Arrested for what?" I asked.

He answered, "Why, for burglary. Jerry was walking home last night about ten o'clock when he heard a shot fired in the neighborhood and a man dashed by a few minutes later. Two cops ran along and arrested Jerry, saying that he was the man who had held up a grocery store. From the police station he telephoned to me this morning to come and get him out on bail."

"Well," remarked Frank, calmly, "now the police station will be full of vermin, as he has slept there one night already. Those poor prisoners will have a hell of a time from now on."

"But what are we going to do about it?" Leo asked.

"Do nothing at all," Frank answered.

"Do nothing!" I exclaimed.

"No," said Frank. "This isn't the first time Jerry has been arrested, but as far as I know they have never been able to sentence him yet. Since it is quite alien to his nature to appropriate other people's property, they will not be able to convict him."

"But he might rot in jail all the time before the trial comes up," I objected.

"Oh no. They will let him off," Frank said. "The police are extremely thick-headed; they will find a much better man to take the thief's place. Though they generally don't know the difference between a hobo and a criminal, they won't keep Jerry too long."

"But they may railroad him into jail," I protested.

"Railroad your grandmother!" Frank exclaimed. "They will never do any such thing. It is too expensive to keep a man like him in jail. They will let him out, and we will have to feed him."

Hearing the house stirring upstairs and knowing it was time for me to begin my work, I urged Frank and Leo to get out.

"All right," said Leo. "I will go to the police station and see what can be done."

I spent the day at work and in great excitement. But I could not find the boys anywhere, either by telephoning or by going to the rooming-house where we had that common bed. Later in the evening as I was reading, I heard the same scratching on my window pane, and in stepped Jerry.

"Hello, I thought you were in jail," I said. "What happened, have they bailed you out?"

"No," he answered, "they let me off."

"Do Frank and Leo know?"

"I don't know. I haven't seen them since morning."

"But," I said, "they had gone out to get you out on bail."

He said, "Well, I suppose they are looking for the bail yet. In the meantime the police have found the real thief, and as they did not need me any longer they let me go."

"Did they treat you badly?" I asked him.

"Well," Jerry answered, "the State is always stupid, you know. Whenever the State puts its hand on you, it generally leaves you a little damaged after the transaction. Until you have abolished the State, my boy, you will have no individual freedom. Can you imagine two fat-heads dressed in certain uniforms behaving as if they were Almighty God and taking liberties with any citizen walking in the streets? But it is no use, we will have to abolish the State, the Church and Society before we have peace and freedom on earth."

"Where do you think the other two are?" I asked.

He said, "I don't know and I don't care. Probably they are sleeping in our room. But let's go and see, maybe the two fools are wandering about looking for someone to go bail for me."

We went out and wandered around Fillmore Street and lo and behold, from two different street corners Leo and Frank were haranguing the crowd. I heard Leo say:

"Until you abolish the State, we will have no freedom. The State is an absolute authority in a given territory. As long as there is so much authority there is little freedom in that territory. So, ladies and gentlemen, let us imprison, abolish, put to death the arch criminal that preys upon humanity—the State."

At the other corner, standing on an inverted tub, Frank was saying:

"Ladies and gentlemen, I have already proved to you that life isn't worth living and it is much less worth living if we have to be sandwiched between the Church and the State; between the upper and the nether millstones. We are not only ground exceedingly small, but we are really ground down to nothing. I believe in the sanctity of the individual, and you, as individuals, have just as much chance to be yourselves as a cow has when she is giving milk. If you only had the wisdom of a cow, you wouldn't be what you are."

The audience applauded him with great gusto. He saw me and Jerry in the audience, and said:

"Now I will stop, and my Hindu comrade will pass the hat."

So I passed the hat, and we made two dollars that evening. Frank was glad to see Jerry and so was Leo at the end of his harangue. Leo was rather more surprised because this was the first time he had come anywhere near an experience of jail for himself or his friends. Jerry held forth on his jail experiences. He said:

"The first time I was jailed it was in Chicago. I was caught with a lot of laborers and put in prison, but later on they found nothing on me so they let me out. That one month of my incarceration was full of brilliant thoughts. When you are busy you don't think much. But in jail each criminal let me know his life experience between whispers and broken sentences. Then I learned that it is just as easy to get accustomed to live within four walls as it is to live in space walled up by the sky. Prison does not make criminals of us, but it does make perfect animals of us. I don't see, however, why we should have any prejudice against animals. Perhaps it is very interesting to be an animal. However, it is rotten to adapt one's self to everything as animals do, no matter what befalls them.

"The second time I was arrested it was for white slave traffic. It was in a brothel where I had gone to look up a young girl I had seen walking the streets at night. I had a talk with her. I brought her to my house and gave her room and shelter, but her procuress came and wanted to take her away from me. 'Return my girl to me,' she demanded.

"And I told her to go to hell. In a week's time I was arrested for indulging in white slave traffic and the case against me was perfectly clear. I was the man, according to the evidence of the prosecution, who had brought this girl and sold her into prostitution. Then later I had violated my contract with the procuress and took her with me for further transactions. They found me red-handed, as the girl was with me being made ready for further transactions in another city of the Middle West, as they were prepared to prove.

"Well, the thing looked pretty bad, and I knew by this time, in spite of all innocence, there was no escape for me. I tell you frankly that you may be as innocent and harmless as a dove, yet you cannot escape injury from the malicious people that live in this world. These people do harm as naturally as a snake secretes poison in its fangs.

"So in course of time the trial came off. The jury was selected: three rich merchants, one clergyman, I think, and the rest were nondescripts of one profession or another. The evidence came off with a great deal of ease. I was identified by two people—a railroad conductor and a negro porter of the brothel. They corroborated each other in saying that I was the man who brought this girl to the brothel and that after bringing her there, I removed her from the place for further business, as I have already mentioned.

"The thing looked perfect. I could see no way of putting a hole in the evidence of the other side. The district attorney raged like a gigantic bull who had seen a red flag. I thought the jury would blow up under his raging, but they sat there like twelve vultures, waiting to see which way the corpse was going to fall. The judge was very much like an old undertaker who had lost all interest in corpses and death. To him it was the routine of business. No wonder he looked glum. The whole thing was solemn like a gigantic funeral service in which I was the man lying in the casket. The vast ritual of law poured upon me like holy water. I tell you frankly, if you want to be buried at all, be buried in a law court. Elsewhere rituals are not as alive.

"However, I knew my mind. I said to myself, 'There is only one way to puncture their evidence and that is, to play cat and mouse with the evidence of the Negro.' So I said that I wanted to cross-examine the Negro. The district attorney smiled, signalled the Negro to get into the witness stand, and I began:

"'When did you see me come in?'

"He said, 'Last October.'

"I said, 'What date of the month?'

"'Don't know, sir. It was Friday.'

"'What kind of clothes did I wear?'

"'Don't know you wore any clothes, sir.'

"'What did I look like?'

"Negro: 'Like a gentleman, sir.'

"'Can you recognize a gentleman when you see one?'

"The district attorney: 'I object.'

"The judge: 'The objection is sustained.'

"'Do you remember when I came what I had in my hand?'

"'Nothing, sir.'

"'Do you remember how I entered the house?'

"'You sneaked in like a skunk, sir.'

"'Did I smell like a skunk?'

"District attorney: 'I object.'

"The court: 'The objection is sustained.'

"'After I came into the house, what happened?'

"'Nothing, sir.'

"'Are you quite sure I went in all alone?"

"Negro: 'Yes, sir. No one that am a gentleman goes with somebody else. I see all kinds of gentlemen come and go, but I never see one come with nobody else.'

"'Then you are sure I had no one else with me?'

"'No, sir.'

"'Are you sure I had no one with me, man or woman?'

"'No, sir.'

"'But you said in this evidence that I brought this young lady with me.'

"'So I did, sir.'

"'Then, which is true? Did I come alone or did I come with the young lady?'

"'I don't know, sir, you got me all mixed up.'

"'Can you tell me who taught you to tell the lie that I brought the young lady there to your place?'

"The Negro was going to say who it was when the district attorney got up and objected, and the court was overruling the objection when I said: 'Your honor, I do not need to pursue this matter any further. This shows that the poor Negro does not know his own mind and I wouldn't be a bit surprised if he was tutored to give this evidence.'

"Then I also cross-examined the conductor. He, however, remained consistent in his statements all through the cross-examination and the only point he yielded was that he was not sure where I got on the train with the young lady. And he was not sure whether I got off at Englewood or La Salle Street.

"I wanted to go on with the case a little further and examine one or two more witnesses, but I saw that it was useless. I asked the Negro to come on the stand again, and he broke down and cried. He wailed, 'Please don't ask me no more questions! I ain't done nothing. It is them white folks that put all them notions in my head. I ain't done nothing.'

"So the jury returned a verdict of not guilty."

"What happened to the girl?" asked Leo.

"Well, she had a varied career afterwards. I took her under my charge and brought her around to a sense of decency. I taught her reading and writing, that is to say, reading and writing worthwhile English. Then I took on a job for two years as a bartender in a saloon and the money that I made there I spent in giving her a commercial education."

I said, "What a filthy thing to do, to sell things to put an end to men's minds. You didn't sell alcohol?"

Jerry answered, "How do you know that your ideas do not smother people's minds just as much as alcohol does. Only one you call ideas, the other intoxication. That is all the difference."

"But what happened to her after that?" Leo asked.

"Well, she became a lawyer's clerk," Jerry answered. "Then happened the usual thing. The lawyer fell in love with her, divorced his wife and married her. And thus ended the career of a girl who might have grown into something noble and great. But women have a fear of greatness. They prefer the security of marriage. Why? I don't know."

"What do you know about women?" I asked him.

"Very little," admitted Jerry. "In my time I have known great women, too, like Louise Michel. I have met Mrs. Bridges Adams of England. I have heard Annie Besant lecture. I have known young ladies, aspiring, unaspiring, animals, intelligent, all sorts, and all as comrades and friends, and I find the majority of them quite incapable of madness. It takes a man to go mad over an idea. That is why the majority of the prophets of the world have been men. Women somehow see into the relation of things; men see things as they rise up in prominence, one upon the other. And it is their power to give prominence and their devotion to the most prominent thing which drives them mad. And if they are not mad, they are so inspired that they look mad."

Frank said, "I don't agree with you at all. Women are not at all different from men, but men like to think that women are different, that is all. I once met a woman with whom I was in love. She was rich and I was poor. She was a capitalist and I was not. It was during one of my Socialist harangues from a soap box at a street corner that I saw her. She came again and again to hear me.

"One day she invited me to dinner and I came to her house. She was a well-to-do widow. As we grew more and more intimate I introduced her to the writings of Bernard Shaw, Anatole France and Mirabeau; and I could see her mind grow as grow the trees in the tropics, swift and green. But you see I was in love with her, but she was not—at least not to the extent that I was. So one day I made a fool of myself. I proposed to her and told her that I wanted to marry her. She said, 'No,' and I asked her the reason.

"She said, 'A woman or a man may marry as often as they like, but a time comes in one's life when an experience of love is as insipid as overripe fruit. I am weary of love and people that make love. They are so selfish that they think they want to give themselves away. You see I have grown really unselfish. I have no desire to give myself away.'

"Then I said to her. 'But you are hurting me.'

"She answered, 'Love makes us so vain that everything hurts us.'

"I left that night. Within a week I got a letter saying: 'I am going to be married to So-and-So. I want you to come to the church and be one of my witnesses.'

"I gasped in consternation, 'No!'"

"Yes," said Frank. "She behaved exactly as a man does, for I too was married in a month."

All three of us exclaimed, "You, married!"

He said, "Oh yes. I was married, loved, and then given up for good."

"What do you mean?" I said.

"I married a lady in Virginia. I lived with her about eight months, when I found out that there was no more love between us than there was between myself and this lamp-post. We were victims of the dull monotony of sex. Having realized that one day, I left. No one knows what happened to her. It is sixteen years now. Yet I feel that perhaps if I went back to Virginia, I would find her the same sweet, kind, somewhat unintelligent woman, trying to be happy in a world where life is not a case of happiness, but a means to knowledge."

"But is it a means to knowledge?" asked Jerry.

Frank said, "I don't know. It seems so to me."

"No," said Jerry. "The orientals are right. Life is a problem involved in will. How to express one's will is the problem of life, while we in the West have made of life a problem of knowledge. And look at the mess we are in. The whole Western civilization is a civilization of ignorance and blindness. In the East they don't go in for knowledge, so their ignorance does not hurt them. They express their will and that is all; or they don't express their will and that is enough. Yes, we are the victims of the most elusive hopes in the universe."

"Then do you advise me," I asked, "to go back to India?"

"Yes, I do," said Jerry.

"But," I said, "what about the future of humanity?"

Jerry said, "Let humanity alone. Humanity is the sewer through which we are all passing. We do not see why we should improve the sewer unless it clogs our passage too much. If I were you, I would go back to India and sit under a tree and dream my dreams. In the West we are commercializing our dreams. Even the utopias are being made so practicable that nobody has any interest in them. You have at least the power to dream. We haven't got that much even."

"But what about anarchy? Aren't we going to bring anarchy into this world?" I asked him.

Jerry answered, "Anarchism is an attitude which only the healthy souls can acquire and since it is an attitude of the soul what is the use of making it a problem of education. The whole Western mind is imbued with the idea that you can teach something. You can no more teach a man anarchism than you can teach a man how to angle for stars."

"But what about your third jail experience, Jerry?" Leo asked him.

"My third experience in jail was really an authentic one. Has any one of you committed a theft?" he asked.

Leo and I shook our heads sadly acknowledging our own unimportance. Frank, who was older, was not as vain as we were. He asked Jerry, "What did you steal?"

Jerry answered, "I forged a check and stole five hundred dollars."

"Were you arrested?"

"Yes."

"How long were you sentenced?"

"I was sentenced to a year's imprisonment."

"What did you do it for?" I asked.

"Just for experience. Besides, I needed the money."

"What could you need such an amount for?"

"You remember the procuress who wouldn't let go of the girl from that brothel because she had paid for her?"

"Yes."

"Well, after the girl departed from town I gave her five hundred dollars which the girl owed her. I knew that was the best thing because the girl was married and I did not want the procuress to follow her up."

"And whose check did you forge, Jerry?"

"The owner of my saloon. He was dead drunk and I made him believe that he signed his own signature and gave me the five hundred dollars."

"But you said you were sentenced to one year's imprisonment?"

"I was, because he denied from the witness stand that he had written out his own signature and given me five hundred dollars."

"So you served a year in prison, Jerry?"

"Yes, and it taught me one thing. Man is incapable of great love. That is why he is so fond of pity. You know why Christianity dominates half of mankind? Not that it loves Jesus Christ, but it loves Christ's pity for all that suffer and are heavily laden. Man isn't made for the sublime rôle of being a lover, but he lives for the beggar's alms, the pity of the world. And it is the poorer side of Christianity that is the religion of half the world."

"But as for you, Jerry," Leo asked, "didn't you love this girl?"

"No, I pitied her," he answered. "I did not love her. I do not think I can love anything but the squirrels and the birds in their cages."

"But I remember," I accused him, "that I saw you at the dog fancier's who sells birds over there. I have seen you every now and then save up money to buy a bird or squirrel and then free him in the park."

"Yes, it is the one thing I enjoy most," he admitted. "Whenever I have money I go and buy one of those poor captives and set him free. O God, what is it that keeps us from being noble lovers? We are always pitying, pitying, all of us and everything that we do!"

I had now come to the conclusion that if I stayed in the city I would pretty soon be giving up my job, to talk and wander with the boys. I saw that talk wouldn't do. I must go and earn money and finish up my college work and although Frank had promised me forty dollars a month I did not want to take his money. So I decided to try my luck at work in a factory out over the Bay. However, I wanted to spend a whole fortnight with the boys before I went off, so we decided that Frank would stay across the Bay where he worked for the Socialist paper, and I would share the bed with Jerry and Leo.

The following day, after doing some odd jobs for twenty-five cents an hour, I came to the rooming-house at half past five to go to sleep. I saw Jerry standing in front of the house, his face wearing an expression of great annoyance.

"Hello, Jerry," I called out. "What's the matter?"

"I have given it all up," he answered.

"Given what up?" I asked with not the faintest idea of his meaning.

"I have given up that bed," Jerry answered firmly.

"What do you mean?" I said, "I came here to sleep."

"You can't understand, I suppose, but to me it is terrible," he almost wept, "we were using the bed all the time. Either you were sleeping or I was sleeping or Leo was sleeping. Think of it! The poor bed never had any rest. So I gave it up. One should not exploit even a bed. Now I am going to buy some more squirrels and set them free in the park," he concluded.

That finished me. I said, "All right. You have the right to give up your bed. We are all free. We owe nothing to each other. I am going up tomorrow to the factory."

He agreed that this was the wisest thing to do. "You see, Dhan," he said, "you come from another civilization, and you are not tough enough to stand this bumming. You must be brought up in shelter. This hard life of freedom is hell. Hungry, without a coat on one's back, the men yet love their life of freedom. Well, goodbye, go to your factory. Let's see each other once in a while."

So I went to the factory in a town called Cannington. We were to work twelve hours a day. The factory ran twenty-four hours a day with two shifts, one at night and one during the day. I had secured the position of assistant chemist through correspondence with the company.

When I went to the laboratory the first day, the chief chemist said, "Will you analyze this sample?" Then I had to confess that I knew absolutely nothing of chemistry but that I must keep this position to help me through college. The chief did not seem to think much of this new assistant but agreed to give me a trial.

"Instead of twelve hours a day, you had better put in fourteen at least," he advised. "You may learn to memorize the analyses, and if you do it an hour a week you may pass for a sugar chemist. Most of them don't know sugar chemistry, and those that know sugar chemistry don't know anything else."

So I learned all kinds of strange words: polarization, evaporation, carbonization, carbonation: strange, fantastic words like strange animals coming out of the Himalayas. My chief was a fine man. He was arrogant, vulgar, uncouth but very kind. His heart was as big as an elephant. At heart he believed in union hours, but when he came to speak he always voted for twelve hours a day.

So the factory rumbled on. It whistled at six in the morning, it whistled at noon, at six o'clock in the evening, and at midnight. Into the belly of this monster crawled men and women like roaches walking about in a hot kitchen. It was ghastly. I had never heard so much filthy talk from anybody as from some of those factory laborers. I have known the vulgarity of the people of my country, but it was picturesque vulgarity. When a person called another names, he said: "O thou granddaughter of a he-ass." But when a modern industrial man swears, he neither reverses the sex of the person he is swearing at nor does he give the person such a delectable ancestor as a he-ass.

It really was terrible. In a community of four hundred laborers the majority of whom were not married, they had a red light district, where there were three prostitutes. Once in a while one could see three or four rows of men going in and out of these houses. What a vast difference between the vices of the East and West!

In the East a prostitute is a woman of art. She knows how to sing and dance. After all she is a dancer and singer. She attracts by more than sex. But here in this vile factory town, human flesh and human souls were sold like hogs or oxen.

One very hot day after a night of work I was wandering through the town, quite worn out from lack of rest and too hot and tired to sleep. I took a walk through the town and I went into a drug store to buy something or other, when a loudly dressed woman smiled and bowed to me and went out.

I met her another day about a week after our first encounter. She said, "Come and take a walk with me."

She and I walked into the park and sat down and talked for two hours, I telling her a little of my life in college and she telling me the tragedy of her life and evidently thankful for the genuine interest I showed in the hurts a fellow creature had suffered. I learned that she had been a student in a well-known woman's university, but the sordid story of her fall, I need not recount.

"But you know it doesn't pay to be unhappy very long," she ended. "In truth, I can't be unhappy at all. I talk like this and I feel as if I am not telling the whole truth. Well, I think I had better be going. It is now half past five."

She got up, shook my hand and walked away. I knew it would be soon six o'clock and that the human beast must rage in the pig-sty of sex after the day's work. I went back to the factory to work.

In the factory I had a set-to. My chief called me and told me I had been seen walking with a dirty woman in the streets.

"What of it?" I said.

"Well, nobody recognizes this girl when they see her," he answered. "Suppose it's true that quite a number of them recognize her in her house, that is where she is to be recognized, but the man who recognizes her in the streets of this town is a dirty dog. And if you go about with her again, we will fire you and you will have to leave town."

"But a great many of the men know her," I insisted.

"Yes," he agreed, "but they never speak to her outside of the district. It would be a hell of a community if she were to associate with everyone out of her place. Pretty soon there would be no distinction between them and respectable women. Look out, pretty soon you will lose your job. Maybe some one will smash your head, too."

The colossal impudence and vulgarity of it became more and more evident to me. Man after man came to me and said that if I were again seen speaking to that woman on the street, I would be run out of town. I must not speak to her out of the place "where she belongs."

This made me hot. I said, "I don't know where she belongs. It takes fellows like you to know that."

Suddenly the wheels stopped—it was about midnight. The factory stopped rumbling and the monster just lay lazily panting. All the lights went out and everywhere little lamps were lit to investigate what was the matter with the engine.

"Why has she stopped?" they asked each other.

It turned out that a lizard had crawled up into the dynamo room. Not being versed in engineering I could not understand what they told me. In that darkness with little lamps between us, I recited to the chief chemist: "We are such stuff as dreams are made of—and our little life is rounded with a sleep."

"What the hell makes you talk poetry?" was my chief's rejoinder to this.

I answered him, "Sorrow is the source of song and singing relieves sadness."

"Poetry don't buy you bread, you nut," he said.

I answered him, "No, but it sustains your spirit."

"It does, does it?" said the man of action. "Well, as you are so incompetent in chemistry and so damn competent in poetry, why don't you learn chemistry to buy you bread? Poetry keeps you ragged and poor. You look like a starved rat. Do you ever think of that?"

"But what is the good of it all?" I asked him.

"Say, if you are going to talk like that," he answered, "you had better hire a hall and then you can talk all you want. When I went to college I wanted to study chemistry, but I found that I had to study poetry even if I wanted a degree in chemistry. They make you go through Shakespeare, Dickens, and all those guys, and what a mess they make of it."

"But don't you see," I said, "if they give you Shakespeare as a task you never love him, and if you have to pass examinations on a thing it becomes so dull you acquire a loathing for it that hurts beyond the grave."

The whistles blew, the electric lights were turned on and the monster groaned, panted for a few moments and then the whirl and the tumult of wheel and engine began.

The next day—I don't know why—I gave up my position at Cannington, and took the first train to San Francisco.

V

What is the Answer?

When I reached San Francisco I found that the college had opened already. I paid my fees there and found a good job under a Negro woman, waiting on tables, washing dishes, keeping the house clean. My zest for anarchism was coming to an end. I began to see that there was nothing to do but to find a new philosophy, something that had little concern with the material future of mankind. It was during this period that I began to rediscover India.

We had reached the fall of the year nineteen hundred and twelve. Things, both political and otherwise, were fermenting in India. Batches of Indian students began to come to America for wisdom and knowledge and the more I saw these men coming, the more I grew convinced that they were coming through a desert to slake their thirst with the waters of a mirage.

By now I had drunk the dregs of the Western civilization. I found it had its vulgarity, its bitter indifference, its colossal frauds. It has made just as many mistakes as India has in her time. And yet there was something constructive in both of these civilizations.

All these Indian students I met were nationalists. They wanted to free India. As if a politically free India meant an India traditionally and uniquely herself! Bitter quarrels ensued between myself and many of these Indians. These people thought that if India had factories and a government as well as an army and navy of her own, she would be one of the civilized countries of the earth.

Take the typical Indian revolutionist. Many people remember him in San Francisco. He wanted to cut the throat of every English official just as he wanted to cut the throat of every Indian traitor. He meditated such a gigantic slaughter that he seemed to me like an epic poet of death. He contemplated vast holocausts as magnificent offerings to the god of Patriotism. He devised ingenious plans to blow up garrisons of English soldiers as a disinfectant and a preventive of political hells, and once in a while he would grow lyrical about the joy of belonging to a free people. He imagined very suave massacres, and delicate assassinations.

One day I told him, "Look here, why should we supersede British massacres by our own, except that our own may be a little more radical? Theirs are only practical and utilitarian."

He said, "Their massacres are continuous. Ours would be only momentary and purely unavoidable. There is economy in killing. If by killing a few hundred English you could create a free India, then it must be done. I am looking at it from the standpoint of economy."

"That is what wearies me so much," I answered. "Your economy is so scientific, your massacres are so hygienic, that I have no more interest in them than I have in conic sections. All your assassinations are mathematical and well founded in fact and if they really came off they would be more cruel than the massacre of St. Bartholomew or the Russian pogroms. These at least had a religion and a ritual to make them bearable."

To this he said, "You talk like a slave. Not only have the British conquered us, but they charge that rebellion is unholy, and a destructive profanity. If you could see their soulless railroads piercing through the sacred places throughout India, tunnelling the Himalayas like a monster driving its tentacles into the vitals of your body and sucking out your life blood! If you only realized and imagined these things vividly you would not be sitting here talking like a fool."

"It is true that this industrialization of Asia is terrible," I admitted. "It is sucking out the life blood of Asia, but your quarrel is not with the British nation, but with Western capitalism."

He shook his head and said, "No, if we had our own people exploiting the natural resources of our country, and if we had our own army and navy, we would be spending our money in our own country. Our money wouldn't be spent in England and Europe as it is spent by giving salaries to European officials. Think of it! If our dividends were paid to Indians in India, how much better off our country would be."

So he wanted to overcome imperialism by a nationalism just as crude and as greedy. I told him so, and added, "I do not like to interpret you this way."

"I don't care how you interpret me," he answered. "Your interpretations are tainted with pro-Western bias. You are a slave."

"But why," I asked him, "don't we think in terms of two classes, the possessing class and the dispossessed classes, throughout the world? These two marching against each other are to my mind the forces of the conflict. I cannot make out much difference between imperialism and nationalism."

To this his rejoinder was that I talked like a soulless Socialist.

"I am not a Socialist," I said. "I hate Socialism. Socialists only want to create a new authority in the place of an old one. What I want is to create a sense of freedom in people's souls. Then all will be well."

"How dare you talk about souls when the bodies are starving to death? How dare you insult a man dying for lack of food with your talk of philosophy?"

"Yes," I agreed, "you are right, but one must talk of souls after the body is fed. It is the most important thing according to our ancestors."

He was becoming more and more provoked with me and now sneered, "What do you know about your ancestors?"

I tried then another way and asked, "Tell me, how can I serve my country?"

He answered, "By holding your tongue."

However, I saw all kinds and shades of opinions regarding nationalism in India. The most pathetic one that I came across was the following from another Hindu. I shall call him Nanda.

I said to Nanda, who was a recent arrival from India at that time: "Look here, I have been living in the West nearly three years now, and I am quite convinced that I have nothing to learn from the West. What we have to do is to go back to the belief of our ancestors that there is nothing wrong with this world. Whatever is wrong with the world is wrong with us first. So as we purify our own hearts and become holy men ourselves, the problem of the world will be solved. We must become like the gods. Then we shall want nothing because we have overcome our sense of want within ourselves. If we control our appetites by our soul, we will have very little to fight for and against. By changing ourselves we automatically change the world.

"You remember when Buddha walked by the harlot's house, the house became purified because a spiritual human being walked by it. So I think, Nanda, that the road open to us is not the way of the college, but the way of the spirit. And I do think in this matter our country can teach the West."

Nanda replied, "I agree with you that we have a spiritual wealth which is more important than our material wealth. The material wealth that we have underground in India combined with the cheap labor that lives above the ground is the thing that attracts Western exploitation. Western capitalism finds in those two factors enough inducement to come to India and to tear up the whole system of personal relationship founded on domestic industry, substituting in its place this terrible Western 'civilization.' Peasants are driven from their fields where they worked eight hours a day to other people's factories where they work twelve hours a day. When a peasant breaks the ground he sings, when he works in a factory he spits and swears."

And I added, "In order to overcome this great industrialization of the East by the West, we must overcome ourselves first. If we want to fight this gregarious gluttony which the West brings to us, we must overcome our own gluttony. If we free ourselves from ourselves first, we will be able to save Asia from the West, I think, almost automatically."

"Well," said Nanda, "that is true. India has material resources and untold riches, and think of her subjective background of spiritual wealth. If the West could only tap this wealth! But how to give it, that is the problem. If we come to the West and say, 'We have spiritual wealth—take it from us,' the West will say, 'How can you be spiritual when you are a conquered race? Races that are truly spiritual have their own economic system and are masters of everything.' How are we going to meet this question of the West?"

I said, "I don't know. Do you?"

Nanda said, "The West will never accept the spirituality of the East until by force we free our country from any Western domination. In order to give the spirituality of India to the modern barbarism of Europe we must beat them at their own game. We must go through the necessary step of nationalism and nationality. Until we have a victorious India free from all foreign control and domination no proud Western nation will ever care to listen to our spiritual talk."

That afternoon with the thought of Nanda in my mind I went over to visit Jerry. What Nanda said troubled me. Must the East also be hooliganized in order to give the West its spiritual truth? Was it necessary?

At this time Leo and Jerry and Frank were living together and from San Francisco Frank was editing his Socialist weekly. He had shaved off his beard, and now that I did not need his money, with some saving, he had managed to buy for himself and the other two, new suits of clothes. When I came in they were all sitting together and talking.

Frank asked me, "Dhan, how long have you owned that grey suit?"

I said, "Two years."

"Well, when next week's salary comes I will go and buy you a new suit," Frank said; but Leo objected, urging immediate action.

"They will let you have it on credit," he said, "and you can pay them next week. Dhan looks like the devil in that suit, it looks like the national flag of India. I can recognize it from any distance."

So we went to the tailor's and they gave me a ready-made suit. These were the first new clothes that I had worn in nearly three years. I was so proud of them that I felt hurt because people didn't look at me. They always used to look at me when I came in with the other suit.

We adjourned to a pinochle joint, and discussed philosophy. I told Jerry what had passed between me and Nanda.

Frank said, "You know, Nanda must be a brilliant fellow!"

"I don't like it," said Leo. "These brilliant Indians, in order to overcome the intellectualism of the West, are creating a rival intellectualism of their own. I can quite imagine Gladstone or rather Lord Salisbury saying solemnly, 'We are forced to conquer the world in order to give it the benefit of the spirituality of our nation. England must take over miles of "undesirable territory" in order to give other nations her spiritual institutions, her moral wealth, and her Shakespeare. These Indians ought to know better than to tell us that they have to conquer us first in order to give us their spiritual wealth.'"

Suddenly Leo turned his gaze on me and asked, "Do you notice how the Western ruler is conquering India mentally? You are thinking in his terms!"

"That is true," said Frank, "but I think there is an aim to this whole thing. You know the Jewish history. The Jews are an oriental people. If I remember their book clearly, the greatest events came to them when they were either in exile or in captivity. Their important prophets arose when they were persecuted, and their greatest prophet came when they were groaning under the Roman rule.

"There is a curious thing. When Jesus was asked whether the Jews should pay taxes to Caesar, he said, 'Give unto Caesar what is Caesar's.' By this he meant to say to the Jews that it was easy to placate their Roman lords by sacrificing a few ounces of matter, gold or silver, which had no importance. But it was their relation to God which was of real value.

"Now I think," Frank continued, "that the Indian should look at it in that way. He must not try to overcome Western materialism with a rival materialism of his own. The Indian who is an oriental must give an answer like Christ's—'I am so busy with my spiritual business that I have no time to pay attention to you who are demanding something material.' And it is not a humiliation to belong to a conquered race. The people that are most humiliated in this Indian-British transaction are the British. They are damning their souls by exploiting a race in the name of British liberty. They are selling liberty as a prostitute sells her body.

"The Indian, on the contrary, is selling very little, so if I were to choose between the conquered or the conqueror I would prefer to be the conquered. At least your soul is saved. Give your spirituality to the British as Christ gave his to the Romans. And it is because you are conquered that you are spiritually sound. If you were not conquered you would not be spiritual."

I looked at Jerry because I knew that he did not have Frank's systematic way of thinking, but he had a mind which like the lightning cleaved the sky.

Jerry said, after a long pause, "It is all so unnecessary. You may have a free country, but it does not follow that you have a free soul. To give a man a vote in a so-called free country is like giving a lantern to a blind man. What use is it? We are in this world to destroy our blindness and then see the light. And these fools come and want to make a ghastly mockery of blindness by giving it a vote. Because every blind voter has a vote which is his lantern, it does not necessarily follow that he will find the road to freedom. By stringing blind men to blind men, you do not create vision. The sophistry of these Indians is very brilliant, and like all sophistry has its uses, but it always misleads the young, and the young love to be deceived."

And Leo asked, "And the old, Jerry?"

"The old live by deceiving the young. The men work; the women work and spend. Every folly thus is balanced with irony, and every irony in turn begets its folly. This is the description of that brilliant chaos we call the universe."

"But, Jerry," I said, "what is the answer to all this?"

"There is an answer somewhere, but he who has found it, as some of your old Indian sages have done, knows that the little chalice of the human word cannot hold it."

VI

In California Fields

It was about this time that I ran into a bludgeoning of Socialists by the police force. I do not seem to remember now what the cause of it was, unless that the Socialists had become too prominent in the main cities of California. Of course we did not belong to the Socialist party, in fact, even to this day, I do not know why anybody belonged.

One of the chief leaders of the Socialists in town was a blind man named Jones. He was a very keen thinker, but being blind, he did not meet very many people, and did not go out at all. He had a lovely wife whom he bored by always talking about "the system." He seemed to think that if a thing could be traced to the capitalist system, it could be cured, so no matter what came up—nationalism, militarism, anarchism—he would always search and examine the subject till he found its relation to capitalism, and then with a sweet smile on his lips, he would conclude, "it is up to you to abolish the system."

Here was this brilliant fellow looking forward to a catastrophe which he thought must come, though he did not like direct action. In fact all he liked was prominence and power. He was one of the first men who gave me an inkling that Socialists are no different from capitalists. Everyone wants to express his sense of power. Everyone wants to preach his own truth. Everyone wants to assert his own authority. This is the aim of each human being, no matter what group he belongs to. So I heard the voice of egotism when blind Jones talked to me. Though his eyes were shut he was just as blind as those who could see.

Jones had arranged a protest meeting through his henchmen. In this protest meeting two things were to be done. One was to protest against the closing of the street corners to Socialist speakers, and the other was to initiate Mr. Jones into some office. I have never found out what the nature of that office was.

By seven o'clock the hall was full of men and women and boys and girls. The motion was put before the house that Mr. Jones should take the chair, which he did. With a great speech, the blind man announced that the proceedings would commence. There was a lot of talk by many speakers, some of whom had a good many nice things to say about the chairman.

Then Jerry got up and addressed the meeting, saying: "Ladies and gentlemen, Jones has been put into this office. By whom? We have always had a great deal of love for Nietzsche's *Uebermensch*. We do not mind the rule of nature's superman, but it is a damn shame that we are going to be ruled by Jones's undermen. Why should his people engineer this meeting and put him in the chair?"

At this there were shouts of "Shut up." "You are an Anarchist." "You don't belong here."

So Jerry sat down.

Then another man got up and made a speech and said that the Socialists and Anarchists are the same people; that if they would spend much less time quarreling with each other and would devote more time to fighting their common enemy, the capitalist system, the world would be better in ten days.

Jerry shouted: "I wouldn't make the world better for a single Socialist; I prefer to make it worse."

"Take him out," someone shouted.

"Will someone put the resolution before the meeting?"

So the resolution was put; the assembly resolved that the authorities in control of the city government were treating the Socialists like an outlaw community. "To all of which we do solemnly protest," and so forth and so on.

Hardly had the resolution been passed when a terrible shriek arose from the rear end of the house, and the crowd moved like cattle in a flaming cowshed. Policemen's clubs were rising and falling and men and women were hurrying about, diving under chairs and tables. Above us sat Jones on the dais, a blind man who could only hear, but see nothing.

Next to me there was a woman, and next to her was Frank. Suddenly, from nowhere, we saw a club rise in the air and come down over the woman's head. I put out my hand and Frank dove right into the woman and pushed her out of the way, and the club came down on Frank's head. The next thing I knew was a shooting pain on my shoulder and then another and still another that gave me a sense of pleasing blackness all around. Even then I saw more clubs falling. I remember vividly a club descending on Jones's head, but quickly Jones was pushed aside before the club reached him. Now a fierce darkness possessed me and I was lowered into an abyss of perfect calm.

When I woke up I found I was in an unfamiliar room, but I heard Frank's old familiar voice saying, "Are you awake, Dhan?"

I said, "Yes, what was it?"

"Oh, you are remembering? You will remember all pretty soon."

I asked, "Was anyone killed?"

"No, those fellows never kill," he answered, "they just hurt."

"How are you, Frank?"

"My head is broken again, but it has saved a pregnant woman from being beaten up," he answered.

I said, "Thank God for your head, Frank.

The next day when we saw Jerry he had a broken club in his hand. "I broke this club on a policeman's head," he told us. "He had hit me on a vulnerable spot. But I finished his arrogance. He fell supinely with one stroke of the club."

"How is Leo?" Frank asked.

"Leo is in the hospital," Jerry answered. "They have broken his arm, but he will be all right tomorrow. This being clubbed is getting to be monotonous. I am going to chuck the whole show and go in for something more varied."

"What do you want?" said Frank. "Do you want to go and live in the Palace Hotel for a change?"

I asked Jerry what started the fight.

He said, "Like fools the Socialists did not lock the doors in the back, and there was no way out in the front. So we were caught between two streams of police coming from two doors, and there was nothing to do but hurl chairs and save one's neck. And the people are so helpless when they are caught in flank attacks. But it does not matter. They all took their beatings soundly, and that in itself is a winnowing of Socialists. Well, let us put out the State, let us put out the Church, let us put out Society, for where there is nothing there is God."

I murmured the same prayer and fell asleep.

The rest of this semester nothing interrupted the dull monotony of life and the even pursuit of living, so as soon as vacation came around I took up out-of-door work. I went out to the country to work with the Hindu laborers. I found them very hard working people, living almost wholly on vegetables, and having in general such a low standard of living that the native Americans were agitating against Hindu immigration on the ground that my countrymen were pulling down the wages and getting all the jobs.

First I worked in the asparagus fields. It was a ghastly performance. We got up at half past three, and before the first faint daylight was visible we were ready for work. We were paid by the piece, and if we filled up a whole box of asparagus we received ten cents. They gave us miles and miles of asparagus rows. As soon as I had knelt down with my knife and cut out one head and put it in the box, there would be another one sprouting before me. Then I would have to stoop again, and it was this continuous picking and stooping that made it a terrible form of exercise. It is walk and bend, bend and walk, from half past four or thereabouts, until seven in the evening.

What used to disgust me so with these men was their love of work. They worked longer hours than any other laborer would dream of working, and it was no wonder the American union laborer wanted to exclude them. They were underselling the Americans in their own fields.

Into these asparagus fields once in a while would come the boss—an American foreman—and he would say, "Hurry up! Hurry up!" goading the human cattle to more energy and more work. Sometimes the men would be so weary that they would go and fetch liquor with which to drink themselves into forgetfulness. Soon I came to see that my countrymen, who had few vices at home, with six months of this kind of work had been reduced to such a condition that they were drinking up their wages in order to forget they were alive. All the old Indian bringing-up was being swept away by a few months of inhumanly cruel work.

There was a Hindu woman in this place. She was in love with another man than her husband, and the two men wanted to kill each other. This was the first time I saw the morality of the Hindu woman give way under the pressure of work, but the soullessness of the job told even upon her.

One day while her husband was working, word came that she had run away with her lover. The husband left us the next day and in a week he brought back his recalcitrant wife. He had given her a terrible beating and now wanted to break her lover's neck. In India this could never have happened, for Indians dare not raise a hand against their wives. But now that work had reduced both the men and the woman to the condition of beasts, they had lost their Indian delicacy. Had they acquired in its place American delicacy that would have been just as good. Alas, the truth was that the men and the woman were thoroughly soulless. She accused her husband in an American court, and succeeded in substantiating her charges of cruelty. He was sentenced to prison. All his relations with life hitherto had been objective. Now he was shut out from the objective world and since he had no subjective background to lean upon, he suffered torments.

Once I went to visit him in prison. And he said, "I see no green grass. There is no sun. There is nothing. O God, if I could only kill myself. I cannot endure it any longer!"

As if God had heard him, within a year he died of consumption. When this news came to the wife, she left her lover. And it is said that she took ship for India, but never reached home. She committed suicide at a Chinese port.

From the asparagus fields a little later I went to work in the celery fields. We were all working together, and as most of the people knew no English I interpreted for them whenever the occasion arose.

One day as we were all busily working, some people in blue caps with red bands around them approached us, but we went on working and paid no attention. When you work on the soil too long you pay no attention to many things that pass. So we all went on with our work without regard to the visitors. But they evidently were not disturbed by our lack of interest in them, for one of them called out in English: "Brother, have you thought of your sins?"

The men asked me, "What does the fool want?"

I translated to them: "He wants to know about your sins."

"Our sins?" they replied. "It is none of his business. Our sins belong to our priest and ourselves. Who is he?"

I asked the man who they were. He replied that they belonged to the Salvation Army.

I translated this into our language saying: "They represent the Militarism of Nirvana."

The workers rose as one man, dropped their tools automatically as if they had seen a ghost in the dark.

Then the Salvation Army man said, "We bring you peace."

So I told the men, "He brings you peace."

One of the men said, "How can he bring us peace when he militarizes Nirvana? What does he wish with our sins?"

So I asked him in English, "What do you wish to do with our sins?"

"I want to wipe your sins away with the blood of Jesus," he answered.

So I interpreted to them, "He wants to convert us to Bibi Miriam and her Son."

"Oho, so he is the ambassador of the Son of Bibi Miriam," said one of the men. "Ask the brother-in-law what he has done with his own sins."

(Brother-in-law is a term of insult in India.)

I asked him, and then translated his answer: "The Bibi Miriam's Son has wiped away all his sins."

And another of the workmen answered, "If his sins are wiped away, why doesn't he go singing songs of joy? Why does he look for other people's sins like a rat looking for holes?"

I translated as best I could for the benefit of the Salvation Army man.

He said, "Brother, I wish to bring *you* the light."

I translated this to the workers: "He is a purveyor of the Sun."

"Tell him we do not need Bibi Miriam's Son. We have our own Light," said one.

Then I said, "But he wants money."

At this the crowd laughed and an old man said, "Oh, truly he did not come for sins, he wanted our money."

Then one of the younger men said, "Oh, get rid of him. Give him whatever he wants."

So we raised a small collection and gave it to the Salvation Army man and his companion. Then they said a prayer for us before they left. One of the Indians said, "Why do they shut their eyes when they talk to God?"

I said, "Canst thou tell me why we open our eyes when we talk to God?"

And the man laughed and said, "Indeed, that is a good jest."

So we all set to work again.

The work we did was very difficult in that it required much bending over and walking fast on tiptoe through long rows of celery fields, planting, or rather transplanting, plant after plant.

We had an extraordinary boss. He was an Italian constantly swearing and spitting. He seemed to think that if he shouted hard enough at everyone he had done his duty and so we evolved a very clever trick. Whenever he shouted we worked hard and as he stopped shouting we relaxed our speed. As it is humanly impossible to shout all day long, even for an Italian, our boss would leave us after shouting continuously half an hour or so. Then we would slacken our speed and relax. "There he is coming back," someone would shout, and by the time he could see us we were working again at a terrific rate. We nearly always heard him before we saw him for he was noisily drunk half the day and the other half he fretted because he was not drunk.

Then the time came to pick fruits from the trees. This was the most enjoyable form of work. With our baskets we disappeared above the boughs and plucked all kinds of fruits. From our tree tops we would see the boss coming 'way off in the distance and when he reached us he found us working very hard.

Once he stood under my tree when my basket was half full and I was standing on one of the limbs. He began to swear and curse from below and I felt so nervous and so driven to work in a hurry that I tried to do too many things at once. To my dismay the basket fell on the boss's head. A deluge of apples choked the oaths that were coming out of his mouth and to crown all I followed the apples.

I lay flat on the ground waiting for him to strike me but he was knocked unconscious. After a few moments when I saw him lying prone without the slightest movement to indicate that he was going to get up, I raised myself on my elbow and watched. He was lying in a dead faint. I shouted for help. The other workers stopped work and we managed to carry him to his shack and all of us spent half an hour reviving him. It was the most joyful diversion I have ever had while picking fruits.

Later on I worked with the Japanese. Once when I saw this same boss coming at a distance, I said to the Japanese, "Boss is coming, hurry up."

One of them, whose name was Kanagawa, answered back, "Hurry up-o, hurry up-o no good, work too much, all work finished; our job gone. Work slow, and job last, savvy?"

So between Kanagawa and myself the work that should have taken a week lasted a fortnight. We always worked rapidly while the boss was about, so no one reproached us.

From fruit picking we went to hop picking. This time I was with Mohammedans from the northwestern border of India. They all spoke Hindustanee, prayed in Arabic and told filthy stories in Pushtu. The last mentioned trait created a strange solidarity among them. They enjoyed their own vulgarity without divulging what it was all about.

Once they translated one or two stories to me, and that is how I happened to know later on by their snicker and laughter what kind of narrative they were indulging in.

This is one of the specimens of their stories:

A man went away from his home and two years later his wife wrote him that a child had been born to her, and the man felt very proud and showed this letter to quite a number of his comrades. They asked him how could she have a child while he was away so long? But the man shook his head wisely and said, "But I write her letters."

These men were extraordinary. Their religion forbids drinking, so any time one of them wanted to drink, he would have to buy his liquor and go into hiding in order to indulge his appetites. No man knew what the other was doing during these periods of retirement. I, not being of their religion, was invited on more than one occasion to come and have a drink on the solemn promise that I would not tell anyone.

The time came for the fasting of Muharram. They fasted from moon to moon and ate a little at certain appointed hours. Sometimes the fast lasted forty-eight hours. Quite a number of them ate in stealth, but a very large majority went without food for two days and worked hard in the hop fields eleven hours out of twenty-four.

With the hop pickers there was a priest whose name was Hadji, since he had done a *hadj*, that is, a pilgrimage to Mecca. He was the only one who could read the Koran in Arabic. They would not read the Koran from the level where they all sat. That seemed sacrilegious to them. So they piled up bales of hay about eight feet high and then Hadji climbed up there and read from above to the crowd, quite a lot of whom were listening, and quite a lot of whom were playing checkers. This reading was interrupted only the few hours during which Hadji slept. At four o'clock in the morning we could hear his shrill voice calling the faithful to listen, and praying "O Allah, the Almighty Allah, the Compassionate," etc.

But the owner of the hay wanted to take the hay away to the stable to feed the horses, so bale by bale the Koran began to come down to human level. One afternoon we brought two Americans to hear the Hadji read. These Christian infidels very soon shut the book without asking his permission, told him to step off from the bales of hay, and removed all of them from under the Koran. Their excuse was that they had been sent by the owner to fetch all the hay. The consternation among the faithful was something indescribable; but what could they do? The Mohammedans wanted to fight these Christians, but the Christians had revolvers and all kinds of weapons and they had none. So they went about and gathered together more hay and built up a new altar on which the Koran and Hadji were hoisted. Then the reading was resumed.

Once I asked Hadji if they allowed any mercy for the Christians or the Hindus. "Nay," he said, "they shall pass under the edge of the sword of chastisement, and their souls shall be given over to everlasting flame."

And I answered, "That is exactly what the Christians say about the Mohammedans and the Hindus."

He said, "The Christian God only threatens, but our God will do it, so you had better be a Mohammedan in a short time."

I said, "Those of us who go to heaven, what happens to them?"

"They enjoy paradise." He did not give me the description of a paradise of the senses which I had expected of him. He rather described it as a serene place of exaltation.

I said, "Shall we see the face of God in Paradise?"

He answered, "No, even there when we come to the glory of the Lord, our faces will be down in the dust, for He indeed is Allah, the Terrible."

At last the period of fasting was over and the feasting began. The Mohammedans would not buy the American butcher's meat, for animals whose flesh they eat must be killed by having their throats cut and in no other way. So they bought three big rams and after a great deal of prayer and benediction, cut their throats. The poor creatures writhed in mortal pain for a few moments as the blood gushed out and wet the ground.

I said to Hadji, "Why do you kill them this way?"

"It is the way of our Lord; it is in the Koran," he answered me. "We never question such things. We would never eat anything that is not slaughtered this way."

That night they gorged themselves with superb ardor. After the feasting was over they beat tin cans and sang all night. They had one refrain for all these songs, which being translated reads thus; "Your hair is like a panther's shadow. Your eyebrows are like the curve of a hawk's wings."

These Mohammedans had another way of cheating their employers, unique and original. Since it was forbidden in their religion to tell lies they generally employed a Hindu or a Christian to keep their books and at the end of their time there would be found in those books the names of forty men instead of the thirty that had actually worked.

I once asked this bookkeeper why he wrote down such things. He said, "Why shouldn't I tell lies, since if I don't somebody else will, and take my salary away from me?"

But not long after this they found a very clever Mohammedan who could keep books, so they discharged the Hindu. The Mohammedan never entered forty men in the place of thirty in the book. His trick was something very different. Since he could not tell lies and since he knew very little English all he did was to talk to the overseer, and the overseer would interpret his thought through his broken words. Whenever the bookkeeper said thirty, the overseer translated thirty into forty. The bookkeeper would then make a profound bow as if the overseer's word were law, and there was no overseer on earth who could resist that bow.

This form of cheating we later on called "bonus" and we gave the name of "bonus monger" to our bookkeeper. And it is true that the "bonus monger" was a very religious man. He always said his prayers five times a day. He never forgot a single one and said them according to the traditions prescribed in the Hadith and Koran. Before long all were following his example. The result was, I noticed, that instead of working eleven hours a day, they really worked only ten, one hour being consumed in prayer at the employer's expense.

In the next place we went to after we had finished in this hop field, the employer said, "I will give you fifteen cents apiece more, if you cut out the prayer." They all agreed to pray three times a day instead of five.

VII

Spiritualism

I left the hop fields about three weeks before college opened and went back to town to see my comrades. When I reached town Jerry told me that there was a woman who wanted to rent a room free to a Hindu. So I looked up this lady, and she really gave me a room free in her house, and what is more, she asked me to put on my Hindu robe and sit in the parlor one hour a day in exchange for which she offered to give me my meals. I was astounded at this kindness. She never put any hindrances to my coming and going and I ate my meals there whenever I pleased.

This gave me the opportunity of being with the boys, who had by now discovered Bergson's philosophy and were reading William James as well. We spent no end of time discussing free will.

Every evening when I came back to my house I always found the parlor door closed and heard people whispering. Every morning at a certain hour I was asked to put on my Hindu robes and come down and sit in the parlor for an hour. At last my suspicions were aroused and I asked my landlady, "Is there nothing else I can do for you?"

She said, "If someone asks you what you do here, will you please tell them that you demonstrate."

"Demonstrate?" I asked, not having the slightest idea what she meant.

She said, "Yes, materialize, you know."

"Materialize what?" I asked, more and more mystified.

"You know," she said, "the thing that you do in the old country."

"What do we do in our country?"

She said, "You know—the spirit."

"Spirit what?" I asked.

"Why, the spirit of the dead?"

In amazement I exclaimed, "What the devil are they doing in this house?"

She waved her hand and said, "Don't you understand? Didn't Jerry tell you?"

"He told me nothing," I replied.

The woman said, "Why, we materialize the spirits here and ask for messages."

I said, "You don't mean to tell me you are a spiritualist?"

"Of course," she said. "Aren't you one?"

"I don't think I am," I answered.

"Every Hindu is one," she insisted. "Spiritualism comes from India."

"How do you know it comes from India? I have never seen it there," I declared, "except among very questionable people."

She said, "But in America they are very respectable people, people like myself."

"Are you sure you are respectable?" I asked her.

"My Lord, what a question to ask!" she exclaimed, not in the least offended, and continued, "Look here, you come to our séance tonight in this house at eight o'clock and then the medium will be here, too."

So I went to the séance at eight o'clock in the evening and met all the people, who were obviously very ignorant and hopelessly credulous. The medium lay on the table and we sat around her, and pretty soon somebody tapped my head and said, "Here is one who is doubting."

"It is our Hindu brother," someone announced.

I said, "I don't doubt it, I believe it."

Then the medium said, "I am your mother's spirit. Do you remember the yellow-eyed cat at our house?"

I said, "If you are my mother's spirit, why do you talk about cats?"

The medium answered, "It is to remind you that I haven't forgotten anything about the house. What is it you want to know?"

I said, "What is happening in India this minute in our home?"

The medium said, "Everybody has gone to sleep."

I said, "No. It is just the opposite. They are all waking up from their sleep. They are going to work."

Then something hit me on the head with a great bang. The lights were turned on. The medium said, "The spirit refuses to communicate."

I apologized for my stupidity and skeptical attitude, and said that I really believed. "But somehow I don't really see any usefulness in this sort of thing," I added. "This spirit who knows all eternity talks about cats, and what good are cats?"

Then they said, "But why don't you answer a sensible question?"

"But your spirit was wrong," I insisted.

The medium said, "But you must not contradict a spirit."

Well, they let me go and went on with their séance. The next day as I was sitting in the drawing room with my turban on, a woman came into the room. She was about forty, well dressed, and she was introduced to me as someone who wanted to see me.

She said, "Do you remember?"

I looked at her with a puzzled expression. She said, "But you *do* remember."

I puzzled some more in my mind as to what she was reminding me of. "Remember what?" I asked.

"Why, the first time we were in Babylon together," she answered. "You were a priest and I was a temple dancer. You remember? You ruined me and turned me loose in the streets, and for that later on I murdered you. Now we are both on this earth to expiate our past deeds. Now do you remember?"

I answered her question by another, "Are you positive about this Babylon affair?"

She said, "Positive? Why, when I saw you in the semi-darkness the other night during the séance, I went home and the entire fabric of our past opened up in my dream. Now I come to you to say I forgive you. Will you forgive me?"

"But this is crazy," I told her.

She said, "Don't be naughty. I remember you and you loved me, but I didn't love you. But now you are forgiven. In the next world you will be rid of the taint of the past deed. My dream told me, so I had to come and say it to you out loud. Goodbye, brother. I am not a good spiritualist for I believe in rebirth."

She kissed me on the forehead and sailed out of the room.

To crown all, that night about eleven o'clock when I was in bed, I heard a rap on my door and I got out of bed and opened it. I saw nothing, heard nothing. I went to bed again. Hardly had I lain down when there was another rap on the door. I again opened it. There was no one. Now I dressed myself quietly in the dark and lay on my bed. Again another rap. I ran to the door and opened it. Nothing.

As I stood in the doorway I heard someone coming up the stairs. It was my landlady. "Quick," she said, "the spirit is calling you."

"Calling me? What for?" I asked.

"I don't know, it wants to speak to you. Come down." And she spoke with such eager whispers that I could not resist. I hastened into the room where they were having a séance.

I could see very little in that room where everything was wrapped in a shadowy light which deepened the darkness all the more. A voice from the ceiling was saying, "And this I say to you, do not doubt any more. We are going to show you the mysteries that have been kept from you. Therefore go forth on the morrow believing in your sixth sense and make the unknown known to mankind." The voice ceased.

A murmur of adoration greeted this. Then the lights were turned on and I saw a dozen people sitting around a table in the center of the room.

I said, "Why did you call me?"

"The spirit wanted you to hear what it had to say," I was told.

"Did any of you go and rap on my door three times?" I asked. "My door was rapped upon three times successively, but I found no one there."

At once on fire with pleasure, they all assured me that not one of them had left the room for over an hour. "It is the spirit," they declared.

I then asked my landlady, "Who sent you up to my room to call me?"

"It is the spirit," she repeated. "Now you believe, don't you?"

"Yes, I believe," I agreed, "but what's the use of believing such things. I never said I doubted it."

"But don't you believe we live after death?" she asked me.

I told her that I did, "But if you live in the manner of this spirit," I added, "life beyond the grave hardly seems worth while." Then I quoted to them from the *Gita*: "Never the spirit was born, the spirit shall cease to be never; weapons cannot cut it; flames cannot burn it. As man throws away worn-out garments so the spirit throws away worn-out bodies. The spirit is eternal, born of the same intelligent substance as God. It is infinite."

"That is what we believe in," they declared.

"But if you believe in it," I asked them, "why do you talk of the spirit in terms of door mats, wash basins, cats, and broken sticks?"

Before anyone could give me a satisfactory answer, the lights went out and we were again in darkness. A voice said, "I am the spirit of Leonardo da Vinci. What do you wish to know?"

A young girl's voice broke the long silence that followed with, "I am a painter. Will you please tell me how I can be great?"

The voice of Leonardo answered, "You do not have to be great."

Another said—a man's voice, "Will you tell us about alchemy?"

Leonardo said, "It is in my writings."

Then someone said, "Have you seen Dante?"

Leonardo said, "I just left him in paradise."

"Do you know where Shakespeare is?" asked a woman.

"It does not matter where he is," answered Leonardo, seemingly irritated.

Then the young painter girl again asked, "Will you kindly tell me what I ought to paint?"

"Paint with your thoughts," Leonardo told her.

"But I do," the girl almost cried, "and my canvas looks so horrible."

Leonardo dismissed her. "She annoys me," he announced.

Someone said, "Will you please tell us if there is a hell?"

"No," said Leonardo, gruffly.

"Then is there a paradise?" someone else asked, to which Leonardo gave a positive "Yes."

I asked, "How can you have a paradise without hell?" And I got a terrible whack on my head for my question. The light was turned on again. Leonardo had disappeared because I had insulted him.

They asked me if I believed in all this. "Of course I do," I said, "but what's the use of it?"

"There is a great use," they said very solemnly, as the meeting broke up. Yet to this day I have never known what this use could be.

The next day a police officer said to me as I was going out of the house, "Say, are you the fortune teller? You had better look out, the place is going to be raided. We think it is a gambling joint."

I answered him, "It is worse than that. They gamble with the unseen."

"But aren't you the high priest of that crowd?" he continued. "That's what everyone thinks, that you are the Hindu Yogi. You can tell the past, present, and the future. You talk to the spirits. You tell people's fortunes. But I think it is a gambling den. Take my tip, kid, don't go back tonight. The place is going to be raided."

I then went straightway to Jerry and said to him, "What in the world did you mean by putting me in a place like that?"

"I thought I would get you a soft berth," he answered. "They are a crowd of spiritualists and as the Hindus are supposed to be the ancestors of all this weird stuff I sent you over there to help. Your presence has brought them a lot of customers. You have authenticated their claims by being there."

Then I told him what the constable had said.

"Go and get your things and get out of the place then," Jerry advised and added, "I don't mind the unseen being made honorable and real by your presence, but it would not be pleasant to see you behind prison bars."

So I posted back as fast as I could but the police were there ahead of me. One officer was standing in front of the house and two others were leading my landlady down the steps. Seeing this I disappeared and when I did return the following week to get my belongings I met my landlady who accused me of playing the stool pigeon.

I had no idea of her meaning and asked, "What is a stool pigeon?"

"You know, you dirty hound," she said, "but we are honorable people and they didn't find anything on us that was questionable. We gave you a home and comfort. Then you went and betrayed us. You orientals are all alike." With that she flung my bundle at me.

Thus I took my leave. But even to this day I do not know what it was that rapped at my door three times that night.

The experience served to show me that people in the twentieth century are just as credulous as they were in the time of Christ. If the Son of God came to earth today, they would still be asking for miracles and charms. The majority of mankind is spiritually incapable of understanding the larger majesty of God. They want tricks, magic and miracles. Only a few grasp the deep inertia of the sublime, which the mind cannot fathom and words cannot measure.

This year at school we organized a club for the study of Socialism. Hardly had we arranged our program when we were invited by the deans of our respective departments to a consultation. We were told that it was very intelligent of us to open such a club of mental activity, but we were strongly advised to keep our minds open and not to be too hasty in coming to conclusions.

Whether this advice was necessary or not, I do not know, but apparently the youth of America like the youth of India is not trained enough to be able to handle radical thoughts without being led astray by them. I do not know the way out of the dilemma. You cannot learn to swim without getting into the water, as they say. Nor can you become familiar with radical ideas and learn to keep your head straight without danger of complete loss of mental balance.

It was a severe winter this year. There was unemployment everywhere and it was pitiful to see thirty thousand people wandering about the outskirts of the city looking for places to sleep during the night. More than once I have seen people prowling about the garbage cans like mangy dogs. If they saw me, they would run away. Girls and boys, older men and women stood in the rain and sun while waiting for a scrap of food to be handed to them.

It was New Year's night. It had been raining steadily for hours and the streets were flooded. Through the windows of San Francisco's best restaurants we could see women covered with gems and men dressed in evening clothes clinking their glasses and wishing each other happy New Year.

Outside hungry girls were offering to sell their bodies, but the supply seemed to be greater than the demand. I saw a drunken woman step from the sidewalk into the flooded street. As she reeled and fell I ran and picked her up. Then as I helped her, we walked across the street and in the door of a restaurant she turned and gave me a silver dollar, and mumbled a half understandable expression of thanks.

I walked away to where three men were standing under a doorway near an electric lamp. I said to them, "Come on, boys, here is a dollar for you." At first they wanted to have a drink, but they readily agreed to my suggestion to eat seventy-five cents' worth of food and to spend only the balance on drinks. The men were wood choppers out of work, and this was their second meal in three days. Their eyes looked like madmen's.

While I was later walking down Market Street in the rain a girl came to me and said, "Say, kid, can you give me a bed?"

"I haven't money to buy you a bed," I told her, "but you can have mine. It is across the Bay."

"But I want a bed here," she said. "If you give me the money, I will buy one. Besides, it would cost me ten cents to get there and back."

I tried to persuade her by pointing out the chances for a job on the other side.

"What do you think I am?" she asked me. "Keep your dirty job. Do I look like a working girl? No, sir, you won't get me into a house again to peel potatoes."

I said to her, "What are you going to do? You don't look like the other sort."

"I am not fool enough to be the other sort," she answered. "Come, buy me some milk toast in the lunch counter and I'll tell you what I am."

"I have never heard such people—telling all about yourselves," I exclaimed.

At that she looked at me pityingly and said, "Good God, what a fool you are! It's because you are a stranger I can tell you. Do you think I could tell it even to my own brother?"

As we sat down she went on, "I was one of the girls that went to that house during those night séances and I used to go into a spell and tell all kinds of stories. There was a man there and he used to come at night and make a few passes over my face with his hands and then I felt happy and talked my head off. I didn't know what I said."

"So you were the medium," I said. "What happened to you? Wasn't the place raided?"

"Yes," she said, "but there wasn't anything wrong and so no one was held. Afterwards they gave up that kind of work and the man disappeared. Now they run a fortune-telling joint."

She was a forlorn object as she sat before me. "You are soaked with rain," I uttered more to myself than to her, wondering what I could do for her.

"Oh, that's all right. I am used to it," she said. "When the sun comes out I will go to a park. There's a corner there where I'll hang my clothes all up on a tree and they will dry out."

"You just beg for money?" I asked.

"That's all I do. Honest to God, I swear that is all I do, nothing else."

"But you have a head on you. Where are your people?" I continued.

"I have no people," she answered. "My father died in an accident three years ago. My mother married a man with whom she deceived my father. As soon as they were married, they put me out. I saw an advertisement in the newspaper asking for a young, good-looking girl. I went, and became a cloak-room maid in the Palace Hotel. Then I was a waitress, and it was as a waitress that I met the man who makes the spirits talk. Then I had that job until you came and squealed to the police and busted up the show. And now I have nothing, so I wander about and beg."

"But you look more vicious than you talk," I said to her, at which with a "Oh, you make me sick, go to the devil," she suddenly rose from the table and left the restaurant.

I paid for her half-eaten milk toast and went out into the rain.

I had only fifteen cents left. I walked toward the ferry wondering what was the meaning of life. But before I had gone very far I saw the young girl being helped into a gorgeous limousine by a half-drunken man who followed her into it, and I think I heard the man saying to his chauffeur: "Hotel!"

This was America—neither worse nor better than India. All life was a wretched joke and every joke was a sordid travesty. I could bear it no longer. I turned my face toward the East and thought of India.

　　　　　　　　DHAN GOPAL MUKERJI

Epilogue

This was the last of my I.W.W. friends. I got my degree, gave a course of lectures on comparative literature in a college and later began to make lecture tours which brought me into contact with many other kinds of Americans.

I found the United States divided into four psychological groups; the East; the Middle West; the South; and the Pacific Coast. The first section, the East, is in direct touch with Europe and is more like Europe than it is like the rest of America. The second has very little contact with any great external influence. So its culture is more provincial and more indigenous. The South is extremely difficult to make clear. It might seem open to the influence of the Africans, yet that is not the case. It has no great indigenous element. It is full of the eighteenth century European conservatism. But if the climate can be trusted, the Southern men and women will build a tropical culture—sinister and beautiful.

As regards the Pacific Coast, it cannot resist the culture of Asia, as the East cannot be impervious to Europe. Oriental decorations along with Oriental aloofness are becoming discernible elements. In the homes of the Pacific Coast I have found that the people are aloof. They build a Chinese wall of pride around themselves. On the Pacific Coast one also finds something Spanish, not altogether European, but rather Africo-Saracenic in character.

Suppose that the forces of race and culture that I have mentioned go on permeating the whole continent. Then will it be too much to say that in five hundred years America will have a culture unique, magnificent and overpowering? America's tradition is her future. A Hindu, who bears the weight of forty centuries of tradition, is drawn by no country as by America. Europe cannot attract a Hindu. It is not old enough to be benign, nor young enough to be blessed. There is nothing outside of Greece that goes to the heart of a Hindu. There is nothing in Europe that matches the sky hunger of the Himalayas and the fierce fatality of life in the jungles. India has spaces so acrid with loneliness that the greater part of Europe, even Russia, is sweet by comparison, yet Europe is not sweet enough. So a Hindu, who wants to find a complete antithesis to his race and culture, had better avoid Europe and come straight to America.

The future of this country is more staggering than the past of India. A supreme desolation is America's, and this desolation is as alluring as that of the Himalayas. I found in America's air the sharp taste of freedom, not freedom from politicians, not freedom from economic conditions, but freedom from the dead. No dead generations rock the cradle of the new-born here. I felt in America, as in Asia, an anti-human outlook. In Europe, on the other hand, life is homocentric and man is the measure of all things. The nausea of humanity that seizes one in Europe is not present here.

In America, man is what he is in Asia; he is, as he ought to be, an episode, in the life cycle of a continent. He learns that the universe is not homocentric, but cosmocentric. Man's life in America seems like the flight of gnats in a windswept field.

The American is right when he says that he has no time for art and literature. He is a tool, conscious or unconscious, in the hands of a force that is carrying America through a materialistic cycle. Though an individualist, he is not an individual. He has to will the race ideal in spite of his will for his own happiness.

The American woman, too, is chained to the purpose of the race. She has to make her home in a continent fierce with homelessness. In every race it is man that progresses while woman represents continuity. It is the task of the American woman to weave an evergrowing thread of continuity into the changing warp of her life. She cannot, as a woman of an older civilization might do, conquer by her inner sense of rest the restless spaces of America. She has to create a higher restlessness of soul, which by the repose of its energy will give peace. She is already at her task. She is an amateur. She is yet feeling for her part and she makes many mistakes. She may change her religion every six weeks. She may be a humble student of a dozen different schools of art at once. She may pay foreign critics to come and vilify her country. She may allow all the minor poets of Europe to patronize her in her Arab's tent—but all these antics are forms through which the spirit of the race is passing. It is more than the spirit of the race, it is the world spirit.

America is a seed continent. All the world and all the nations are planting their, best and their worst seed in this spring-smitten island. Asia has planted her mysticism, Europe has sown her seeds of diverse intellectual culture, and Africa has offered her innocence.

America is victorious, India is conquered. America is carefree. India is careworn. America lynches Negroes. India illtreats her untouchables. America is abyss-wombed. India has given birth to her abyss. America believes in herself. India is too old to believe in herself. India has caste.

America aims at equality. Thus run the resemblances and differences between the two countries.

The differences are so extreme that the extremes must meet. Both India and America are mad. India has been mad with peace and America is mad with restlessness. It is this madness that has drawn me to them both. Europe is poor fare for my hungry Hindu soul. I want the fecundity of America. I cannot live twenty-four hours a day. I want to live two days in one.

America was discovered in the name of India. Columbus, whose first name was "the Christ bearer," set out for the land of Buddha—for India. He found instead a new land where Christ and Buddha shall meet. The voyage of Columbus ended in a mistake. The next five hundred years will prove that his error was an accuracy of the gods.

THE END

A Note About the Author

Dhan Gopal Mukerji (1890–1936) was an Indian American writer. Born near Calcutta, Mukerji was the son of a former lawyer who devoted himself to music and prayer. A member of the Brahmin caste, Mukerji spent a year living an ascetic lifestyle before enrolling at the University of Calcutta, where he joined a group of Bengali revolutionaries with his older brother Jadugopal. In 1910, Mukerji was sent to Japan to study industrial engineering, which he soon abandoned to emigrate to the United States. Settling in San Francisco, he joined the local bohemian community of anarchists and artists while studying at the University of California at Berkeley and later Stanford. In his time in California, he published two books of poems—*Sandhya, or Songs of Twilight* (1917) and *Rajani, or Songs of the Night* (1922)—and a musical play, *Laila Majnu* (1922). Mukerji graduated in 1914 with a degree in English, married artist Ethel Ray Dugan in 1918, and moved to New York City in the early 1920s. There, he embarked on a career as a popular children's book author, finding success with *Kari the Elephant* (1922) and *Gay Neck, The Story of a Pigeon* (1927), winning the 1928 Newbery Medal from the American Library Association for the latter. Recognized as the first popular writer of Indian origin in the United States, Mukerji struggled with marginalization and racism and regretted his exile from India late in life. Unable to return because of his youthful commitment to revolutionary politics, he supported the Indian independence movement with money and advocacy from abroad. Ultimately, he ended his life alone in his apartment in New York City.

A Note from the Publisher

Spanning many genres, from non-fiction essays to literature classics to children's books and lyric poetry, Mint Edition books showcase the master works of our time in a modern new package. The text is freshly typeset, is clean and easy to read, and features a new note about the author in each volume. Many books also include exclusive new introductory material. Every book boasts a striking new cover, which makes it as appropriate for collecting as it is for gift giving. Mint Edition books are only printed when a reader orders them, so natural resources are not wasted. We're proud that our books are never manufactured in excess and exist only in the exact quantity they need to be read and enjoyed.

bookfinity™

Discover more of your favorite classics with Bookfinity™.

- Track your reading with custom book lists.
- Get great book recommendations for your personalized Reader Type.
- Add reviews for your favorite books.
- AND MUCH MORE!

Visit **bookfinity.com** and take the fun Reader Type quiz to get started.

Enjoy our classic and modern companion pairings!

Printed in the USA
CPSIA information can be obtained
at www.ICGtesting.com
JSHW082340140824
68134JS00020B/1786